Pakistan: A Very Short Introduction

VERY SHORT INTRODUCTIONS are for anyone wanting a stimulating
and accessible way into a new subject. They are written by experts, and
have been translated into more than 45 different languages.

The series began in 1995, and now covers a wide variety of topics in
every discipline. The VSI library currently contains over 650 volumes—a
Very Short Introduction to everything from Psychology and Philosophy of
Science to American History and Relativity—and continues to grow in
every subject area.

Very Short Introductions available now:

For more information visit our website

www.oup.com/vsi/

Pippa Virdee

PAKISTAN

A Very Short Introduction

OXFORD
UNIVERSITY PRESS

OXFORD

UNIVERSITY PRESS

Great Clarendon Street, Oxford, OX2 6DP,
United Kingdom

Oxford University Press is a department of the University of Oxford.
It furthers the University's objective of excellence in research, scholarship,
and education by publishing worldwide. Oxford is a registered trade mark of
Oxford University Press in the UK and in certain other countries

Published in the United States of America by Oxford University Press
198 Madison Avenue, New York, NY 10016, United States of America

British Library Cataloguing in Publication Data

Data available

Library of Congress Control Number: 2021912312

ISBN 978–0–19–884707–6

Printed in Great Britain by
Ashford Colour Press Ltd, Gosport, Hampshire

Contents

Acknowledgements

I was initially uncertain about taking on such a project but when I started reading and doing background research, I realized that there is too much about the politics of the nation-state of Pakistan and in comparison, very little about the history of its land and peoples. It is in that spirit that this *Very Short Introduction* took shape and form.

Along the way, my students at De Montfort University, Leicester, were subjected to some of my interpretations and I thank them for being indulgent. In a way, this project brings me full circle to my own undergraduate days at Coventry University, where Ian Talbot instilled in me an early interest in the peoples, regions, and nations of the subcontinent, and introduced Pakistan to me.

At OUP, I am grateful to Andrea Keegan for her initial persistence and encouragement and Latha Menon and Jenny Nugee for seeing this project come to fruition. I am beholden to the two anonymous reviewers, who provided detailed advice and valuable reassurances, at the very beginning of this project and with the final manuscript.

Upon pulling the final strands together, I asked friends and family to share their views and expertise. For this, I am especially thankful to Yaqoob Khan Bangash, Amajit Chaggar, Ilyas Chattha,

Virinder Kalra, Ali Usman Qasmi, Naila Saleem, and Gulnar Tabassum. They all took the time to read, provide critical feedback, encouragement, and support. Above all, I am indebted to Eleanor Nesbitt and Rakesh Ankit for their close reading of the drafts and the many suggestions they made to improve this work.

With immense sadness, my final note of gratitude is reserved for my mother, who was born near Lahore before Pakistan was born. She would have been filled with joy in seeing this book.

All the responsibility for any omissions, errors, or confusion is entirely mine.

List of illustrations

Abbreviations

AIML	All-India Muslim League, established 1906
CPEC	China–Pakistan Economic Corridor
FATA	Federally Administered Tribal Areas
GHQ	General Headquarters
INC	Indian National Congress
ISI	Inter-Services Intelligence
ISPR	Inter-Services Public Relations
JI	Jamaat-e-Islami—'Islamic Congress', established 1941 in Lahore
JUI (F)	Jamiat Ulema-e Islam—'Assembly of Islamic Clerics', established as JUI in 1945, split in 1988 (F stands for Fazal-ur-Rehman, who leads the party)
KP	Khyber Pakhtunkhwa (formally NWFP)
NWFP	North-West Frontier Province
PML (N)	Pakistani Muslim League (Nawaz), a centre-right conservative party established 1993
PPP	Pakistan People's Party, a centre-left, social-democratic political party established 1967
PTI	Pakistan Tehreek-e-Insaf or Pakistan movement for justice, a centrist political party established 1996
TLP	Tehreek-e-Labbaik Pakistan—a far-right Islamist political party founded by Khadim Hussain Rizvi in 2015

TTP	Tehreek-e-Taliban—Pakistan Taliban, umbrella group based along the Pak-Afghan border
UNDP	United Nations Development Programme
UP	United Provinces (of British India)

Pakistan

Chapter 1
Progress of a dream

The date 23 March 2020 marked the eightieth anniversary of the 'Lahore Resolution', which was passed by the All-India Muslim League (AIML) at its annual session in 1940. It declared that 'the areas in which the Muslims are numerically in a majority as in the North-Western and Eastern Zones of India, should be grouped to constitute "Independent States"'. This sentence had echoes of a 1933 pamphlet by Choudhry Rahmat Ali, published in England 'on behalf of thirty million Muslims of **PAKSTAN**—the five northern units of India: **P**unjab, North-West Frontier (**A**fghan) Province, **K**ashmir, **S**indh and Baluchis**tan**' (*Pak*=pure, *stan*=land, meaning land of the pure). The 1940 resolution brought full circle a vision first outlined by Sir Muhammad Iqbal in his Allahabad presidential address at the 1930 AIML session. The proposal put forward the idea that the Punjab, North-West Frontier Province, Sind, and Balochistan should be amalgamated into a single state.

Unsurprisingly, the 'Lahore Resolution' is considered to be the bedrock of the movement that culminated in the creation of Pakistan in August 1947. Putting it to the delegates, Mohammad Ali Jinnah, the League's president, in a speech made to an enraptured audience estimated at 100,000, addressed them as 'servants of Islam'. Arguing that the problem in British India was 'not inter-communal, but inter-national', he offered the only solution: 'to allow the major nations separate homelands by dividing India into "autonomous national states". Asserting that Muslims were 'not a minority' but 'a nation', as out of eleven provinces of British India they dominated in four, he demanded that 'they must have their homelands, their territory, and their state'. It was this that would lead, he assured, to a friendly settlement 'with regard to minorities, by reciprocal arrangements between Muslim India and Hindu India'.

This resolution and the speech came nine months into the outbreak of the Second World War, which had momentarily paused political activity in the subcontinent. With Viceroy Linlithgow inviting Jinnah along with Mohandas Karamchand Gandhi, leader of the Indian National Congress, seeking cooperation in the British war effort, this provided an opportunity to Jinnah to challenge Gandhi's 'sole authority to speak on behalf of India'. He would subsequently emerge as 'the sole spokesman' of Indian Muslims; the 'Quaid-i-Azam' (Great Leader) in Pakistan. As he foreshadowed in that 1940 speech, 'it is a dream that the Hindus and Muslims can ever evolve a common nationality...[They] derive their inspiration from different sources of history...different epics. To yoke together two such nations under a single state, one as a numerical minority and the other as a majority, could only mean Hindu Raj.'

Termed the 'two-nation' theory, these words paved the pathway to the creation of Pakistan at the time of Indian independence in August 1947. A little later, on 23 March 1949, marking the ninth anniversary of the 'Lahore Resolution', the progressive poet Faiz Ahmed Faiz in his editorial for the daily *The Pakistan Times* mused, 'the dream is as yet unfulfilled'. Faiz, for whom the bloody end of British India was not the *Subh-e Azadi*—Dawn of Freedom—had articulated the anguish of millions in his memorable verse thus: 'This light, smeared and spotted, this night-bitten dawn; This isn't surely the dawn we waited for so eagerly; This isn't surely the dawn with whose desire cradled in our hearts we had set out...'. Now, he lamented the fact that the ideals implicit in the 'Lahore Resolution' were yet to be realized. Already, so much seemed to have changed, including that Jinnah was no longer alive, having passed away on 11 September 1948.

Much of the last seventy-plus years in Pakistan, and in writings on Pakistan, has been spent in what scholar Farzana Sheikh called 'making sense' of this dream and the efforts at its realization. They range from the novelist Salman Rushdie describing the country as 'insufficiently imagined' in 1983 to the historian Faisal Devji declaring it the 'Muslim Zion', thirty years later. In this span of time, one of Pakistan's best-known citizens, the Lahore-born public intellectual and activist Tariq Ali, once bluntly asked, 'Can Pakistan Survive?' As if in an attempt to answer him, the existing literature has exhausted suggestive epigrams like 'the state of martial rule' (1990), 'eye of the storm' (2002), 'between Mosque and Military' (2005), 'Military Inc.' (2007), 'a hard country' (2011), 'on the brink' (2012), 'a new Medina' (2014), and 'the Pakistan paradox' (2015). These titles have together typecast this Muslim homeland of over 200 million and its diaspora in contemporary global politics.

The spirit of struggle for Pakistan in 1940–7 has thus long since metamorphosed into the spectre of an existential crisis. While internally the people and the regime of Pakistan confront challenges of consolidating a national culture and a political economy, externally the nation-state has, in recent times, faced calls to be declared a rogue state. It used to be the United States of America's most 'allied ally' in Asia during much of the Cold War, from the mid-1950s to the mid-1970s. Two events in 1979 in its western neighbours—the Islamic Revolution in Iran and especially the Soviet invasion of Afghanistan—posed a security dilemma with considerable human dimensions for Pakistan throughout the 1980s, while enhancing its intergovernmental relationship with America. Similarly, with the emergence of the Taliban in Afghanistan in 1994 and especially following the 11 September 2001 attacks on America by Al-Qaeda, Pakistan found itself on 'the flight path of American power', becoming a frontline state in America's 'war on terror'.

On 2 May 2011, Osama bin Laden—the founder of Al-Qaeda and thus a major target for the United States—was killed in Abbottabad, less than a hundred kilometres from Pakistan's capital. His presence there, whether for a few months or for some years, as asserted by the investigative journalist Seymour Hersh in 2015, made it impossible to refute allegations of deception and duplicity concerning bin Laden's exile. Any credibility that Pakistan had in the western international community rapidly disappeared. It is difficult to conjure up an image of Pakistan that is not associated with violent conflict, religious fundamentalism, global terrorism, the army and its agency, the Inter-Services Intelligence, and the country's nuclear weapons. Within the region, Pakistan has been locked in conflict with India since their emergence. This increasingly unequal rivalry, which has seen four wars, extends to economic competition, diplomatic one-upmanship, and sporting battles especially in the colonial games of cricket and field hockey. Matches between the two nations perfectly fit the Orwellian phrase of 'war minus the shooting'.

That Pakistan makes news in the western world only when something bad happens is constantly reinforced by the clichés employed in the international media. Trying to move away from this familiar trope is challenging for writers seeking to convey the complexities of Pakistani society. However, without trying to gloss over or glorify the troubled history of a young nation, the land and its people are more than just a security risk in a seemingly forever failing state. It has a vibrant geography that is home to the Indus valley, the site of one of the world's most ancient civilizations; the Karakoram mountain range, containing K2, the Earth's second highest peak; the Cholistan and Thar desert; the Balochistan plateau and the adjoining Makran arid region; and the Arabian seacoast. Its ancient ethnic peoples, with their seventy plus languages, reflect its rich socio-cultural diversity, rather than its

4

narrow political state project. This multi-polarity and complexity contribute towards why it was so difficult to realize the dream that Faiz alluded to in 1949.

In trying to appreciate Pakistan, this *Very Short Introduction* attempts a *longue durée* history of the land and its peoples and not only a seventy-year snapshot of a new nation-state that emerged from the end of British India in August 1947 to become the first nation-state created on the basis of religion. At the heart of this political idea of Pakistan as a homeland for the Muslims of British India was an effort to create a distinct identity, into which geographically distinct, even distant, territories could meld. It is easy to start in August 1947, when Pakistan (West and East) came into being, but without tracing its diverse and dispersed historical past, it is difficult to appreciate first why Pakistan came into being and second why it developed into this military-bureaucratic complex that lost its eastern wing in December 1971 and is constantly balancing on a tightrope. The longer continuities between the land and its peoples are as important as the shorter changes in the political landscape. The fundamental challenge is to comprehend the political construction of Pakistan, intermingled with prior regional, ethnic, linguistic, and cultural identity(s). The latter provides the historical context, the former its contemporary content.

The land, the people, the politics

When the first census of Pakistan (West and East) was conducted in 1951, the combined population of both wings was 76 million, making it the sixth most populous country in the world at the time. Today, the figure for the western wing alone is 220 million spread over 881,913 sq. km (approximately equal to the combined area of France and the United Kingdom), while Bangladesh (b. 1971) is at 164 million. This makes them the fifth and eighth most populous countries in the world. They are also among the largest Muslim populations, with Pakistan second only to Indonesia, while India has the third largest. In terms of gender, 51 per cent of Pakistanis are male. Just over half the nation's population is concentrated in the province of Punjab. This is followed by Sindh, Khyber Pakhtunkhwa (KP), and Balochistan, which is the largest province but the most sparsely populated (approx. 5 per cent). Among these, the province of KP has undergone a number of administrative changes recently. In 2010, it finally relinquished its rather indomitable and famous colonial name, North-West Frontier Province (NWFP), and in 2018, the adjoining tribal regions bordering Afghanistan, called the Federally Administered Tribal Areas (FATA), were merged with KP. In addition to these four provinces, there are the Northern Areas of Gilgit-Baltistan and Azad Jammu and Kashmir, both of which are sparsely populated and politically separate, though there have been attempts to bring them administratively closer to the National Capital Territory of Islamabad. Indeed, in November 2020, Imran Khan declared that Gilgit-Baltistan would be given provisional status to reflect the aspirations of the indigenous people.

These regions are populated by myriad ethnic and religious groups, in which both the majority and minority communities have connections to the ancient world. This is also visually evident in the streets of Pakistan, as a visitor encounters faces (admittedly usually male) that have Arabic, Persian, Afghan, Tajik, Mongolian, Indian, and Eurasian features. Racially, Pakistan represents this palimpsest of different waves of people moving into the subcontinent and there are a number of distinct groups that emerge from this. The Punjabis, descendants of the Indo-Aryans (associated with Indo-European languages) and deriving strength from their farming and agricultural background, are the single largest ethnic group. Punjab has been economically, militarily, and politically strong and cohesive, both historically and in present-day Pakistan. Being an ethnic majority, the Punjabis have dominated the political and military establishments. After 1947 the nexus between the Punjabis and refugee *muhajirs* dominated, which gradually gave way to a Punjabi–Pathan nexus, crucially excluding the largely Bengali East Pakistan wing prior to 1971. Here, lineage-, clan-, and kinship-based networks known as *biradari* are often more powerful than simply religious or ideological affiliations.

The Punjabis are followed by Sindhis and Pathans, demographically speaking, and their kaleidoscope of ethnicities and regions is complicated by additional internal layers of language and religion. While the official name of the country, adopted in 1956 and cemented by the constitution of 1973, is the Islamic Republic of Pakistan, it is more diverse than the name suggests. In his aforementioned 1940 speech, Jinnah had been confident that the establishment of Pakistan 'will far more adequately and effectively safeguard the rights and interests of Muslim and various other minorities'. On the verge of his achievement, on 11 August 1947, he reaffirmed this recognition in a much-quoted passage from a speech delivered to the Constituent Assembly of Pakistan:

> ...Even as regards Muslims you have Pathans, Punjabis, Shias, Sunnis and so on, and among the Hindus you have Brahmins, Vaishnavas, Khatris, also Bengalees and so on...You are free to go to your temples...your mosques or to any other place or worship in this State of Pakistan. You may belong to any religion or caste or creed...that has nothing to do with the business of the State...In course of time Hindus would cease to be Hindus, and Muslims would cease to be Muslims, not in the religious sense, because that is the personal faith of each individual, but in the political sense as citizens of the State.

These words, and the spirit behind them, continue to agitate the country and remain a source of tension. However, much more difficult to erase is the national flag of Pakistan, based as it is on the flag of the All-India Muslim League (Figure 1). It has a vertical white strip on the left-hand side, which is an everyday reminder that the state has a commitment to protect its minorities

1. **Flags and paraphernalia for sale to celebrate Independence Day.**

alongside the majority community, which is represented by the dominant green. Despite this, religious persecution of minorities (approx. 7 million people) has only grown in the decades since Jinnah's death, giving rise to ghettos that both insulate and protect. Pakistan's population is 96 per cent Muslim, with an overwhelming majority of the Sunni sect, but also including the Shi'as, the Ismailis (a Shi'a branch that emerged in the 8th century), and the disputed community of the Ahmadis. Among the rest are Christians, Hindus, and Sikhs, whose minuscule numbers complete this religious mosaic. Moreover, while officially Pakistan's national language is Urdu, it is the mother-tongue of less than 10 per cent of Pakistanis. Many millions more speak Punjabi, Pashto, Sindhi, Balochi, and Saraiki.

Thus what, from the outside, appears to be a homogeneous country is, upon closer inspection, a more complex society in which regionalism, ethnicity, faith, language, *biradari*, class, and gender come to the fore and recede in any given circumstance.

8

This often-volatile intersection of people produces multiple contradictions in this country, and underlying this is a strong sense of religious nationalism. Given the layered influences that comprise present-day Pakistan, it is remarkable how the state apparatus and its ideology has, over a relatively short period of time, managed to achieve this mono-religious nation-state. Underneath it, the land and peoples of Pakistan are more than Islam, with a far more textured past and present than they are usually credited with. It is furthermore a young country with an average age of mid-twenties. This aspiring demographic, in keeping with worldwide trends, is class-conscious and consumption oriented. It is desirous of networks and experiences, which takes its dreams beyond political boundaries.

Chapter 2
The ancient in the modern

Attempting a long history of Pakistan, there are worse places
to begin than the *Five Thousand Years of Pakistan: An
Archaeological Outline* by R. E. M. Wheeler, published in 1950. Its
preface noted that the book was intended to present 'the imposing
material heritage of Pakistan' to the outside world. An equally
important purpose was to preserve this inheritance for
future generations of the new-born nation. Wheeler was the
director-general of the Archaeological Survey of India from 1944
to 1948 and, thus, found himself in the middle of that tumultuous
period which saw the birth of Pakistan. He took up an advisory
role in the new state, helping to organize its archaeological
department and establish a national Museum in its capital, Karachi.
He became the first president of Pakistan Museums Associations
and played a mediating role in the partition of their historical
heritage between India and Pakistan. Of course, the title of his book
is itself a 'wilful paradox', for Wheeler argues for a 5,000-year
history for a nation just born. Considered state propaganda, the
book set out to trace a long history of Pakistan and Wheeler
followed it by writing another book, *The Indus Civilization* (1953),
that celebrated the major sites of one of the oldest civilizations in
human history, now located inside one of its youngest nation-states.

The legacy of Wheeler's mission is mixed. The sites are there, and
his name is preserved in the history textbooks of Pakistan as the

country's founding archaeologist, but one wonders how a modern-day Wheeler would be viewed in Pakistan, with its identity struggles. Much later, another book, *The Indus Saga and the Making of Pakistan* (1996), followed, taking forward the archaeological vestiges laid out by Wheeler. Its author, Aitzaz Ahsan, politician and lawyer, attempted to uncover the 'true bedrock of Pakistan's national identity... buried under the glaciers of myth' by dividing the history of this legendary age of Indus from the everyday realities of a shared memory between India and Pakistan. Ahsan claimed that the Indus had remained 'independent of and separate from India' for 5,000 years. He alludes to two distinct regions—the *Indic* region of India's Gangetic plains, and the *Indus* region of Pakistan. In doing so, Ahsan continued the reaffirmation of the idea of 'two nations'. However, ancient topographical boundaries, migrating people, and shifting and changing languages rarely observed the constraints of modern hard political borders.

This chapter follows Wheeler's outline, from the Indus to the arrival of the first Arabs, albeit in a fragmented way, for the regions that make up modern Pakistan. The aim is to give but a glimpse of their diverse historical continuum that increasingly goes under-remarked and unremembered. The material and cultural connections and confluences of these, through the ages, belie the image of a modern monolith, whose history is as multi-layered as its neighbour's, just as India's populist politics now share a strong smear of narrow nationalism.

The Indus Valley Civilization

There is little disagreement that one of the earliest civilizations the world has known flourished in and around the basin of the Indus river and its tributaries, in the present-day Pakistani provinces of Sindh, Punjab, and Balochistan. From around *c.*3200 BCE to *c.*1300 BCE, there thrived in phases a civilization, later named after the river, whose first and famous discoveries were

بسم الله الرحمن الرحيم

HARAPPA MUSEUM

INAUGURATION CEREMONY OF HARAPPA MUSEUM WAS PERFORMED

BY

KAZI ANWAR-UL-HUQUE, S.PK., S.Q.A.,

MINISTER FOR EDUCATION, HEALTH, LABOUR AND SOCIAL WELFARE,

GOVERNMENT OF PAKISTAN

ON SUNDAY THE 26TH MARCH, 1967.

2. **Inauguration of Harappa Museum, 26 March 1967.**

made at Harappa (Figure 2), in Punjab, and Mohenjodaro (the mound of the dead men), in Sindh. Harappa, the identifier site by which the civilization is also known, is located near the Ravi river, one of the Punjab tributaries of Indus. Archaeological excavations began at these sites in 1920–1 and slowly lifted the lid from a heritage that has eventually amounted to over 1,000 sites, with 400-plus in Pakistan, spread over almost 800,000 sq. km and including all the four provinces of Punjab, Sindh, Balochistan, and KP. These discoveries established that the start of settled civilization and urban culture on the subcontinent was contemporaneous with those in Mesopotamia (Iraq), Egypt, and China. In fact, from Mehrgarh, Balochistan, there is evidence of farming communities dating back to the 7th millennium BCE, hinting at a prehistory of Harappan sites.

Of these excavated sites, it is Mohenjodaro in Sindh, with its distinctive citadel mound comprising the 'great bath', 'granary', and 'college of priests' as well as a bronze female figurine famous as the 'dancing girl', which has become emblematic of this civilization. Similar to Mohenjodaro, Harappa's citadel, cemetery, and granary have become iconic. This long and diverse culture, distinguished by its typical red-and-black pottery, terracotta cones and cakes, standardized bricks, and copper artefacts, is found in a network of early, proto-urban villages, mature and fully-fledged urban cities, and late, declining towns. The level of architectural planning found in these two sites was unparalleled in the ancient world.

The full breadth and depth of that civilization is a phenomenon still being explored. The Indus Valley Civilization is said to have begun to decline around 1900 BCE and, in 1953, Wheeler suggested that the invasion of an Indo-European tribe, the Aryans, had been the reason. However, this theory has since been challenged and, alongside this, it is argued that natural disasters like floods, rising coastline, desiccation, and man-made disasters like over-exploitation of environment led to a definite, if gradual, de-urbanization. Thus, as their archaeological traces thinned, their place in this historical canvas was taken over by the oral narratives of the Aryans and their texts. The Aryans, who arrived in the upper reaches of the Indus region around 1500 BCE, brought with them their sacrificial religion and language, Sanskrit. The *Rig Veda*, the oldest among their oral narratives, was composed sometime between 1500 and 1000 BCE. Consisting of a variety of hymns which had been compiled by about 1000 BCE, it and related texts known collectively as the Vedas were put together around present-day south-eastern Afghanistan and Pakistani Punjab: the region of *Sapta-Sindhu*—seven sacred rivers mentioned in the *Rig Veda*. The later Aryan texts were composed further east in the Indo-Gangetic divide and the upper Ganges valley, thus providing an unwitting basis for Ahsan's two-region theory.

The cultural corpus of the Aryans formed a precursor to the Vedic ideas and practices that would metamorphose into the

Brahmanical socio-cultural order, feeding into present-day Hinduism. Contrary to the 19th- and 20th-century invocations of an 'Aryan race', these Indo-Aryans emerged from the speakers of a subgroup of the Indo-Iranian branch of the Indo-European family of languages. Remnants of these people and language still exist in Pakistan; indeed, many of the rural technologies, architectural designs, and social ordering that exist today can be traced back, albeit via dotted lines and notwithstanding state amnesias, to these earlier civilizations of the Indus valley.

Gandhara, Ashoka, and Buddhism

The period between *c*.1710 and 200 BCE saw the flourishing of the so-called Gandhara Grave culture. The Ghaligai cave, a rock-shelter excavated in the 1950s–1960s, was found to contain engravings, paintings, inscriptions, and carvings—'rock-art'. Located in the Swat valley along the rivers Swat and Dir, it is thought to be associated with the hunter-gatherer Indo-Aryans, before they settled down to agriculture. While both the late-Harappan sites and later Vedic societies shifted east and south towards and beyond the river Sutlej, Balochistan and the north-west saw the emergence of one of the six early iron age cultures of the subcontinent around *c*.1100–500 BCE. Evidence of iron age settlements can be found in Pirak, Balochistan, and Sarai Khola.

The ancient capital of the Gandhara region of north-west Pakistan, Takshashila (Taxila), was a major centre of trade and learning (Figure 3). Discovered in the mid-19th century, Taxila is one of the important archaeological sites in the world but, while the excavated site is sizeable, it only represents a fraction of the ancient site; the majority remains buried, undiscovered. Situated strategically on a branch of the Silk Road, atop Bhir mound, the earliest historical city of Taxila was established by the Achaemenians in the 6th century BCE. Collectively, the different sites of Taxila (Saraidala, Bhir, Sirkap, and Sirsukh) represent an evolution of urban settlement through more than five centuries.

گوتم بدھ کے حالاتِ زندگی

LIFE OF GAUTAMA BUDDHA

BIRTH 563 B.C.
⟶
DEATH 483 B.C.

3. Displays of Gandharan art, Buddha and his life at Taxila Museum (est. 1918).

Excavations at Bhir mound had established occupation plans, street settlements, civic planning, houses, drains, shops, courtyards, stone-works, and terracotta reliefs dating from the 3rd century BCE.

The decline of the Achaemenid Empire (550–330 BCE), which originated in ancient Persia and had extended into the Indus basin, saw the rise of Alexander the Great (356–323 BCE), who knocked on the doors of the subcontinent during his campaign of expansionism and conquest. Gaining control of Gandhara and its capital Taxila, Alexander marched into Punjab. Waging one of his last major battles, Alexander defeated King Porus (r. 326–315 BCE) in the Battle of the Hydaspes, which not only left him wounded but was also one of the costliest battles fought by his army of Macedonians. From the detailed Greek histories, we get a contemporary sense of the geographical breadth of his invasions and of the resistance to them.

Alexander left behind an empire which stretched from Greece to the Indus, but internal conflicts and tussles among his successors allowed Chandragupta Maurya (r. 321–297 BCE) and his mentor, the political philosopher Chanakya (Kautilya), to expand the Mauryan Empire from the Ganges plain towards the Indus valley. The Mauryan Empire controlled most of modern South Asia from its capital Pataliputra (present-day Patna in Bihar, India) from c.324 to 187 BCE. Today, it is remembered mostly for Chanakya's treatise on statecraft, *Arthashastra*, and for the reign of the emperor Ashoka, Chandragupta's grandson, who vastly expanded the Mauryan Empire and spread the religion of Buddhism throughout the subcontinent and beyond. In Shahbaz Garhi and Manshera (both in KP), major rock edicts of Ashokan inscriptions have been found. They give an account of the infamously bloody battle against the kingdom of Kalinga (present-day Odisha, India) which famously led Ashoka to renounce war and convert to Buddhism in c.263 BCE. Remnants of Buddhist history are still scattered around much of north Pakistan like hidden gems, but they are largely neglected, with few attempts to preserve this (non-Islamic) history.

In Takht-i-Bahi in Mardan, KP, there is a large Buddhist monastic complex which, appropriately for an area situated at a cultural crossroads, gave rise to the so-called Gandhara school of art, architecture, and especially sculpture between the 1st century BCE and 5th century CE. Buddhism flourished under the Indo-Greeks, leading to a cultural syncretism with the Hellenistic culture during the Graeco-Bactrian Kingdom. This Graeco-Buddhist school is an early example of the coming together of subcontinental themes and Graeco-Roman styles. Working with stone, blue schist, green phyllite, and later stucco (lime plaster), the school specialized in images of Buddhas. On the other hand, the Swat valley has produced a number of Buddhist sculptures that have stylistically been linked to the Parthian art of Iran. Indeed, when the great Chinese Buddhist monk-scholar Faxian (Fa-Hsien, 337–422 CE) travelled through Gandhara, passing Taxila, Peshawar, and Bannu in 399 CE, he found Buddhism flourishing from Afghanistan to Punjab.

Travel, trade, and people

The Grand Trunk (GT) Road that forms a horizontal artery cutting through north Pakistan (and India) can be traced back to the Mauryan Empire. For over 2,000 years, this road has linked the people of Central Asia to East Asia, moving ideas as well as goods, and allowing cultures to interact, influence, and merge into each other. In medieval times, the road was upgraded considerably under Sher Shah Suri (r. 1538–45) and then by the British in the 19th century. Although the GT Road is divided by international borders, it still provides energy and vibrancy to much of north Pakistan. While the GT Road forms a horizontal link across the subcontinent, the mighty Indus river (one of the longest rivers in the world) cuts through Pakistan vertically. Running through the heart of Pakistan and stretching almost 2,000 miles in length, the

Indus connects and nourishes people from the Kailash range of the Tibetan Himalayas to the province of Sindh before it flows into the Arabian Sea. Etymologically *Sindhu* is the early name for the Indus in Sanskrit. It became *Hindu* to the Persians, from which the name *Indós* travelled to the Greeks and *Indus* to the Romans. Thus, the land of Sindhu/Indus gave its name to the civilization and the people living there, around, and beyond. It is much later that this *Hind*, the region, became associated with Hinduism, the religion, creating a complex interplay of river, region, and religion.

As is the case for much of modern Pakistan, the Persian Gulf provided the main area of long-distance trade for the Harappans. Internally, south Balochistan, coastal and upper Sindh, Cholistan, the central Indus plains, and Punjab were connected among themselves as well as with neighbouring Rajasthan and Gujarat (Kutch and Kathiawar) in present-day India. Then, there were the land routes connecting north Afghanistan with Multan via the Gomal plain and the Taxila valley and south Iran with Mohenjodaro via the Bolan river and the Quetta valley. South Turkmenistan, the Oman peninsula, Bahrain, and Mesopotamia have all yielded Harappan objects. Conversely, lapis lazuli from Afghanistan, jade from Turkmenistan, and tin from Kazakhstan were among Harappan imports, during its mature phase from *c.*2600/2500 BCE to *c.*2000/1900 BCE. This then was clearly a thriving trading network along one sea route and two land routes: north to Afghanistan and West Asia and south to Iran and Mesopotamia.

Ancient north-west India, which is largely in present-day north-west Pakistan, has historically been the gateway to the subcontinent via the Khyber Pass. Apart from Taxila, the other great city of the north-west was Charsadda, located 29 km from Peshawar, in KP. Both Taxila and Charsadda were strategically situated for trading and military purposes, with routes running towards the Kabul valley via the Khyber Pass and the Kashmir valley to Gilgit and Kashgar (present-day Xinjiang, China). Charsadda is the ancient city of Pushkalavati (or Peucelaotis/Proclais), whose people are said to have revolted against Alexander. Except for the British, most other entrants to the subcontinent have come through this corridor, and each has left an indelible mark on the landscape and the people. Subsequently, the Turks, Persians, Afghans, and Mongols left their traces, and in the process, strengthened the links with central Asia, bringing not only marauding armies and material trade but also mixing the people culturally. Still later, Sikhism emerged here in the 16th century from the then-thriving wider *Bhakti* (devotional theism) movement in the Gangetic and Punjab plains.

Thus, with the intermixed ancestry as well as agriculture, customs, and concerns evident from the ancient and medieval histories of this region, the creation or cleansing of a mythical past for contemporary political convenience becomes problematic. It is both dangerous and difficult to read history backwards, if not impossible to undo centuries of 'intermingling' with the drawing of a line in 1947 and barricading of the new border, although, alas, both sides seem to be making a mean and mighty attempt at it.

Spread of Islam

The very idea of Pakistan was only possible with the spread of Islam into the subcontinent. In the year 606 CE, the present-day provinces of Punjab and Sindh were under the reign of Harshavardhana. He ruled until 648 CE and a historical source for his period is the account given by the Chinese Buddhist pilgrim Xuanzang (Chen Hui, 602–64). Xuanzang spent thirteen years travelling in the subcontinent (630–44), having entered it in the time-honoured manner at Peshawar, from Kabul. He went to Charsadda and Taxila, Sialkot and Lahore, Multan and down the Indus to Sindh, before turning south-east. Upon his return, he wrote *Da Tan Xiyu ji*, a unique glimpse into the India of the early to mid 7th century, a time when an Arab naval expedition was arriving on the Sindh coastline, followed by attempts to conquer Makran, the semi-desert coastline of Balochistan.

In 711–12, Muhammad bin Qasim (695–715), the young nephew and son-in-law of Al-Hajjaj ibn Yusuf, governor of Iraq, succeeded in capturing parts of Sindh and Multan from Raja Dahir (the Hindu ruler of lower Sindh). For many, the history of Pakistan starts with this time and with Muhammad bin Qasim as the 'first Pakistani'. Qasim's reign in the region was relatively short, at just four years, and only extended from Sindh to Multan (along the Indus). Born in the city of Ta'if in present-day Saudi Arabia, Qasim was only 17 when he defeated Dahir in 712 CE. His legacy remains controversial, dividing opinion between those who view him as an invading plunderer who forcibly converted locals, and others who regard his period as establishing a way forward for Islam to thrive in the region. Those people not of the Book were recognized as *dhimmis* (non-Muslim 'protected person' with some rights) and a *jizya* (tax) was levied on them, but they were allowed religious freedom, ultimately avoiding the need for mass conversions in order to rule over the subcontinent.

Unlike Xuanzang's contemporaneous and eye-witness account, the description of events in the conquest of Sindh has otherwise survived in historical record through the 13th-century Persian translation of an older Arabic history, the *Chach Nama*, which tells the story of the Hindu ruler of Sindh. These accounts provide an important insight into these early encounters between Hindus and Muslims, through which first colonial and now contemporary politics is often contested. For instance, James Mill's *History of British India*, compulsory reading for men going to serve in British India, presents Qasim as an invader who created ruptures and constituted a breaking point in the region's history. It is in the colonial period of the 18th and 19th centuries, during which a vast amount of literature was translated and recreated, that we begin to see the history of India being categorized and subdivided into the so-called 'Muslim period' and 'Hindu period', which created lazy and often inaccurate periodization. British colonial rule was also a time of enormous socio-economic change and community rivalry, and tensions were heightened by this growing divisive literature, which turned individuals like Qasim into either definite heroes or villains in equal number.

These early Arab incursions through the Arabian Peninsula were soon superseded by the more successful route of the Khyber Pass by the Turks. The Ghaznavid Empire thrived across parts of Iran, Afghanistan, parts of central Asia, and north-west India. Founded by Sabuktigin (r. 977–97), the Ghaznavid dynasty flourished from 977 to 1186 and started to spread the message of Islam into the subcontinent. It was during this time that Al-Biruni (973–1050), one of the greatest medieval scholars and polymaths, accompanied Mahmud of Ghazni (971–1030) in his famous campaigns to the subcontinent. Starting his travels in 1017, Al-Biruni composed *Kitab al-Hind*, which is an extensive exposition of medieval India and considered to be a foundational work of Indology.

This rich and varied heritage, from the ancient Indus valley to the medieval Indology of Al-Biruni, has however been somewhat of a burden for modern Pakistan Studies, a state enterprise that has framed the production of history in the country since 1971, that is, since the severance of its eastern wing. Its revisionism shows the uneasy meeting of the ancient and the medieval in modern Pakistan, with its aim to showcase a particular, homogeneous, and monolithic nation. But regimes receive, and peoples perceive, myth, memory, and history often differently, if not at odds with each other. Thus, the regional diversities born out of the plural trajectories of *five thousand years* of history of the area now called Pakistan are difficult to erase completely.

Chapter 3
Towards the idea of Pakistan

Forts, tombs, and mosques summed up the presence of 'the
Moghuls in West Pakistan' for R. E. M. Wheeler. These markers of
conquest and conviction have created a physical landscape that is
aesthetically awe-inspiring as well as spiritually soothing. At the
same time, they are provocative and politicized in both the shared
and partitioned history of the subcontinent, where, from the 11th
to the 18th century, Buddhism migrated, Sikhism manifested,
Hinduism strengthened, and Islam became established. Above all,
culturally, it was this period that produced a 'protracted,
hybridized composite' Indo-Islamic identity, in the words of its
eminent chronicler Richard M. Eaton, which was to be at stake in
the politics of the mid-20th century.

From Delhi sultanate to the Mughals

Being near the north-western frontier and the south-eastern
extremity, Punjab and Sindh, respectively, always remained
vulnerable to ambitious neighbours from all directions. In the
north, Lahore was at the heart of incursions and conquests, a
situation which only changed with the third Mamluk king,
Iltutmish (r. 1211–36), who shifted the seat of political power in
the region to Delhi. One of the by-products of shifting power to
Delhi from Lahore was that it rendered Lahore relatively
unimportant for the succeeding two centuries. Power instead

shifted to places such as Dipalpur and Multan, which emerged as cultural and commercial centres, while Ajodhan (present-day Pakpattan) found eminence as the seat of the Sufi mystic Baba Farid (1173–1266). Multan was at times associated more with Sindh, with its Sufi (mystic) cult of Lal Shahbaz Qalandar (1177–1274), than with Punjab, and this is reflected in its 'Multani' dialect and its Uchh market.

To pick up the historical tapestry from slightly before where it was left in the last chapter, Mahmud of Ghazni's raids into the north-west and south-west of the subcontinent between 1001 and 1025 are today either celebrated (in Pakistan) or condemned (in India). Both sides forget that these are emotions and traditions manufactured by the English East India Company (and its successor British Raj) in the mid-19th century. These were colonial attempts to make and write the history of the region they were starting to rule. The Ghaznavid dynasty was of Turkic origin and ruled from Lahore, until the arrival of the Ghurids, who conquered Lahore in 1186 and reached Delhi by 1206. The Ghurids were of Persian descent and began the percolation of Persian cultural and linguistic influences into the subcontinent. Centuries later, in 1987, the Pakistani military gave a nod to their memory by naming its medium-range missiles Ghauri-I-III after Sultan Muhammad Ghauri.

The period that followed is collectively referred to as the Delhi sultanate. Ruling from Delhi, five Turkic-Afghan dynasties (the Mamluk dynasty 1206–90; the Khalji dynasty 1290–1320; the Tughlaq dynasty 1320–1414; the Sayyid dynasty 1414–51; and the Lodi dynasty 1451–1526) ruled over extensive parts of the subcontinent from 1206 to 1526. It is during this period that we start to see increasing cultural synthesis, and the emergence of an Indo-Islamic civilization, reflected in monuments and language, from the lofty heights of the Qutb Minar minaret (named after the founder of the Delhi sultanate Qutb-ud-Din Aibak and now a UNESCO World Heritage site) to the development of the grass

23

roots vernacular of Hindustani (Hindi-Urdu) in the Deccan plains
of north and central India. Attached to the royal court of Alauddin
Khalji (r. 1296–1316), the poet-musician Amir Khusro, considered
the father of Urdu/Hindavi literature, began fusing together
Indo-Persian influences, weaving them through mystic, devotional
poetry. Urdu was ultimately to become the rallying voice of the
Pakistan Movement of the early 20th century. By the mid-14th
century, the Moroccan scholar Ibn Battuta (1304–77) was also
speaking of the Delhi sultanate of the Tughluqs as an Indo-Islamic
empire of 'Hind and Sind'; yet again echoing unconsciously a
variation of the two-region theme.

But it was not until the rulers who have collectively come to be
known as the 'Great Mughals' established their power that
Indo-Islamic culture received state patronage and took root in the
subcontinent. Babur, Zahir ud-Din Mohammad (1483–1530), a
descendant of the Mongol Genghis Khan (1162–1227) and the
founder of the Timurid dynasty, Timur/Tamerlane (1336–1405),
came first, marching across the Punjab to take Lahore in 1524.
Two years later, in the battle of Panipat (present-day Haryana,
India), he defeated the Lodi forces and heralded Mughal control
of north India. What followed was a reign of nearly 200 years by
the Great Mughals, ending with Aurangzeb in 1707. Humayun
succeeded his father Babur in 1530, but his rule was punctuated
by Sher Shah Suri, a Pashtun ruling from his kingdom based in
Sasaram (Bihar, India) and famed for his building of the Grand
Trunk Road.

It was Humayun's son Akbar (r. 1556–1605) who earned the
sobriquet 'the Great', for being a conqueror of territories,
consolidator of states, and creator of a syncretic and pacifist
culture of *Din-i-Ilahi* (a multi-faith religion) and *Sulh-i-Kul*
(peace and reconciliation). He went through the Punjab and up
the Khyber Pass to capture Kabul in 1586, moved his capital to
Lahore that year (until 1598), and again traversed the Punjab,
journeying down the Indus to capture Sindh in 1591. Thus, from

the Hindu Kush mountains to the Arabian Sea, once again, an attempt was made to systematize, centralize, and hybridize the state over these multi-ethnic/religious societies, by carving out *Subas* (provinces) and laying the foundation of colonial and present-day provinces. At its pinnacle, Akbar's subcontinental empire saw a great patronage of art, craft, and architecture.

Jahangir (r. 1605–27) followed his father Akbar to the throne and was, temperamentally, better suited to the dexterity and insight required for the arts than to court politics. In popular imagination, he is better remembered as Salim, through his legendary tragic love affair with Anarkali, a Mughal courtesan from Lahore; there is an equally famous Anarkali bazaar there. The more substantial, if not scandalous, relationship was with his wife, Nur Jahan (1577–1645), who was a widow when Jahangir married her and who earned his complete confidence in his last years to the extent that she emerged in her own right as an empress and had coins minted in her name in 1627. Both Nur Jahan and Jahangir are buried not too far from each other in the city of Lahore, today serving only to attract the occasional tourist.

The reign of Jahangir's fourth son, Shah Jahan, lasted thirty years (1628–58) and this period was the zenith of Mughal architecture, producing mighty and beautiful structures in a new Indo-Persian Saracenic style. The Red Fort and Jama Masjid in Delhi, the Taj Mahal in Agra, and Wazir Khan's mosque and Shalimar Gardens in Lahore all capture the political ability of the Mughals to penetrate all aspects of life (Figure 4). On the military front, expansionism and retreat went hand in hand during his time, and the Mughals' Afghan territories were lost in the 1640s. Henceforth, the Attock Fort on the Indus became the de facto outpost of subcontinental influence towards West/Central Asia.

Aurangzeb (r. 1658–1707) was the next and last of the Great Mughals. He sought pragmatically to pacify the Pashtun tribes beyond the Khyber, and with good reason. In 1667, a Yusufzai

4. The recently restored Shahi Hammam (Royal Bath), built in 1635, Walled City of Lahore.

chieftain of the Swat valley and, in 1672, the Afridis (Pashtun tribe) rose in rebellion. Following this, in 1674–5, Aurangzeb spent a year in the Peshawar region winning over tribes, stabilizing the north-west frontier, and leaving a blueprint that would be followed by the British Indian and Pakistani states alike. The later part of Aurangzeb's reign saw him clash with communities like the Sikhs under Guru Teg Bahadur (1621–75) and Guru Gobind Singh (1666–1708) in the Punjab. Aurangzeb's political ambitions, combined with his personal piety, which saw him endow the grand Badshahi Masjid in Lahore, one of modern Pakistan's most iconic structures, translated into a classic case of 'imperial overreach' and led to the decline of this dynasty.

Sufis and Sikhs

When India and Pakistan were created in August 1947, it was the Sikhs who suffered the spiritual division of their faith. Through the medieval period, with the establishment of Islam on the one hand and increasing alienation with the Brahmanical order on the other, the Punjab region had changed considerably, and these conditions saw the advent of a new religion. Nanak (1469–1539), born in Talwandi (present-day Nankana Sahib, Punjab, Pakistan), preached a new type of message. It was partly born out of the *Bhakti* (devotional) movement, which rejected the rigidity and compartmentalization that both Islam and Hinduism preached. Fearlessly anti-Brahmanical, it found resonance among people in the region and established a following. The Bhakti movement had arrived to meet and mingle with the mystic *Sufis* and, together, both set about challenging their respective orthodoxies, like never before. Personal and popular, direct and simple, poetic and spoken/sung, these movements appeared across regions in different vernaculars.

Distancing himself from both Hindu and Islamic traditions, systems, and institutions, Nanak settled down at Kartarpur (present-day Punjab, Pakistan) on the banks of the river Ravi, and preached upon the importance of meditating in the name of God but at the same time maintaining a family and community life, as opposed to becoming a renouncer. The fluid cultural milieu of early Mughal Punjab permeates the pages of the early Sikh sacred text *Adi Granth*. It includes the devotional verses and hymns of many poets, saints, and Sufis, cutting across religious boundaries, whose names are familiar across the northern part of the subcontinent—names such as Surdas (d. 1573), Kabir (d. *c.*1518), Namdev (d. *c.*1350), and Ravidas (d. 1540), as well as Baba Farid.

The growth of the Sikh faith occurred against the backdrop of the rise of the Mughals and this led to confrontations. While Akbar had cordial, patron relations with Nanak's successors, it was with Jahangir that Sikh–Mughal relations started to decline. The fifth guru, Arjan (1581–1606), gave refuge to the emperor's rebellious son Khusrau and Jahangir ordered his execution. It was, however, with the ordering of the execution of the ninth guru, Teg Bahadur

(1664–75), that Aurangzeb set in motion a fateful clash with the tenth and final guru, Gobind Singh.

During the chaotic period that followed the death of Aurangzeb, Punjab witnessed the decline of Mughal influence and the rise of the Sikhs as strong contenders for political dominance in the region, which eventually led to the establishment of the first Sikh kingdom in Lahore, under the leadership of the young Ranjit Singh, in 1801. This was the pinnacle of Sikh political power, which declined following the death of Ranjit Singh in 1839. Interestingly, and not without controversy, the legacy of Ranjit Singh has been resurrected in Lahore in recent years, including the inauguration of a statue of him as a true 'son of the soil' in 2019; an example of a reassertion of 'regional' identity over 'religious' affiliation.

On the other side of Punjab is Sindh, a 'sleepy backwater' in comparison to the Pathan frontier but, as historian Sarah Ansari observes, a world of '*waderos, sardars* and *pirs*' (feudal landlords, tribal chiefs, and Sufi saints). The province of Sindh has the largest number of Hindus in Pakistan today, with a significant number of followers who are Nanakpanthis (followers of Nanak). A strong characteristic of these regions is the ways in which the institutionalized faith coexists alongside informal allegiances to Sufis, pirs, and gurus. Collectively, Punjab and Sindh saw a rising Muslim piety under charismatic Sufi sheikhs (teachers) and their orders, with two key names of the 13th century being those of Baba Farid in western Punjab and Bahauddin Zakariya (d. 1267?) in southern Punjab. These Persianate Sufis, together with the Persian Wheel (used to lift water in farming), set the towns of Punjab on their way to becoming the region's bread-basket, with a rich local identity. A century later, under Firuz Shah Tughluq (r. 1351–88), Punjab would see the first of its major phases of canal construction from its many rivers, thereby further expanding cultivation and settlement. This was in stark contrast to Sindh, where pastoral communities were suffering from famine in the 13th century.

Much of this region would later witness vast social engineering, which began innocuously in 1831. Alexander Burnes (1805–41), a young political agent of the East India Company, led a mission from near the mouth of the Indus in Sindh, navigating one of its tributaries, Ravi, to reach Lahore. The stated aim was to take a gift of five horses from King William IV to Ranjit Singh. It was played as an opportunity to build alliances, but the real reason behind the expedition was to map the river Indus and its tributaries. This was a precursor to the company annexing first Sindh (1843) and then Punjab (1849)—a far cry from its humble beginnings during Jahangir's reign as seeker of Mughal seals for maritime trade in the Indian peninsula. Within half a century, Punjab would see canalization and formation of canal colonies by the British state on an unprecedented scale, and in another two decades the region would pay its gratitude and debt in blood by contributing well over 100,000 soldiers to the British war effort of the First World War.

Both India and Pakistan, much like the colonial state, have employed these historical periods, selectively, exclusively, and separately, as a political football to chronicle a divided religious history to feed into the creation of two separate nation-states. In doing so, they have either rendered invisible the indivisible cultural connects of a shared syncretic literature or ignored cultural figures, as opposed to men of state. Thus, in addition to those mentioned above, figures such as the poet Waris Shah (1722–98), composer of the love ballad *Heer Ranjha*, and Bulleh Shah (1680–1757) in Punjab, and Shah Abdul Latif (1689–1752) and Sachal Sarmast (1739–1827), their Sindhi counterparts, remain important reminders of the rich interaction between two regions deeply influenced by the linguistic worlds of both Persian and Sanskrit, whose fruit was the Indo-Islamic Urdu/Hindustani and, at the same time, strong regional outpourings in local vernacular folklore.

Seeds of dissent

In the aftermath of the Great Mughals, a number of successors continued to rule in their shrinking, fragmented form between 1707 and 1857, relinquishing power to their regional commanders or *subadars*, and losing the battle against the new imperialist rising and expanding in the region: the British. Their East India Company had received the Royal Charter in 1600, during the last days of Akbar, but the relationship that was cultivated during Jahangir's period was completely severed when the descendants of this Mughal dynasty, under British custody since 1803, were brutally and retributively killed following the recapture of Shahjahanabad (old Delhi) in 1857 by British officers. The last king, Bahadur Shah Zafar, was exiled, and died in Rangoon in 1862, and with that ended the subcontinent's long association with the Mughals. The baton of power now passed on to the British Crown, which took over direct control following the revolt of the sepoys in 1857, which had broadened to other sections of society and spread from Calcutta to Delhi. The Sepoy Mutiny lasted for almost a year and cast a long and dark shadow over British rule in India, with constant fear of rebellion and treachery. Following from it, the British officials began collecting census data in the 1870s, which classified and categorized people, and thus began to entrench communal identities that would ultimately lead to the creation of India and Pakistan.

Whether one sees the uprising against the East India Company in 1857 as a mere 'sepoy mutiny' or a 'peasant-feudal rebellion' or nothing short of 'the first war of independence', the point is that it forms a rupture, in the aftermath of which we begin to see a first wave of the vilification of the 'Muslim other' by the British. The new colonial power was keen to suppress any rekindling of sympathies for the outgoing Mughals, a feeling that was reignited during the days leading up to the rebellion. The Muslim community, dubbed as 'Phantom Wahhabi', were especially targeted and treated with suspicion. Further, the British had already established and harnessed their relationship with the rising Hindu middle class in the colonial cities of Calcutta (Bengal), Madras, and Bombay, which were the first three presidencies in the establishment of British rule in India. In the wake of this existential crisis, the Muslims of north India had to reinvent themselves from belonging to the ruling community to not merely being ruled but minoritized and victimized. It is in this moment that one spots introspection and divergent paths being laid out, paths which would ultimately lead to the formation of two sovereign countries from a multitude of princely states and British-controlled provinces.

In that space of soul searching upon the changing power dynamics among the major communities of the subcontinent, there was much discussion within and between them around how to respond. Some collaborated with the ruling power, others retreated; but among the north Indian Muslims, for rather a long time, there was little appetite to embrace the new western education espoused by colonialists like Thomas Babington Macaulay in his infamous minute on education of 1835, which set out to form 'a class of persons Indian in blood and colour, but English in tastes, in opinions, in morals and in intellect'. William Hunter, a Scottish historian and member of the Indian Civil Service, wrote the book *Indian Musalmans* in 1871. With a focus on Bengal, the book attempts to understand 'a class whom successive Governments have declared to be a source of permanent danger to the Indian Empire'. Elaborating, he directly addresses this in a chapter entitled 'The wrongs of the Musalmans under British rule'.

Almost forgotten today, Hunter was, at one time, considered both the forebear of Muslim separatism and an emblem of the British policy of divide and rule. Four years after Hunter's report was published, the Mohammedan Anglo-Oriental College was established, which would become the Aligarh Muslim University by 1920 and emerge as the cradle of the Pakistan Movement. The establishment of the college by Sir Sayyid Ahmad Khan (1817–98) was a pivotal moment in the awakening of Indian Muslims, as it became the spiritual and rationalist homeland for the Muslim separatist cause. As early as 1887–8, in a series of speeches, Sir Sayyid emphatically and controversially contemplated the consequences of what India would look like after the British left:

> Suppose that all English were to leave India, who would be rulers? Is it possible that two nations—the Mahomedans and the Hindus—could sit on the same throne and remain equal in power? Most certainly not. To hope that both could remain equal is to desire the impossible and the inconceivable.

In trying to understand the emergence of the idea of Pakistan, the late 19th century is crucial in creating these increasingly confrontational, totalizing identities of Hindus and Muslims. Intellectually, the impetus for these rudimentary ideas was being debated and refined by scholars such as Syed Ameer Ali, author of *Spirit of Islam* (1891), and Maulana Altaf Hussain Hali.

Written on the request of Sayyid Ahmad Khan, Hali's *Musaddas-e-Madd-o-Jazr-e-Islam* ('The Ebb and Tide of Islam', published 1879) is considered one of the earliest poetic articulations of creating a Muslim nation. The Urdu poem *Musaddas*, written in the aftermath of the 1857 rebellion, charts the rise and fall of Islamic civilization in world history. Around the same time, in 1882, *Anandamath* ('The Abbey of Bliss') by Bankim Chandra Chatterjee was published but banned by the British. The novel led the Bengali literary renaissance and was part of an aggressive Hindu revivalism, but crucially it was the nationalist movement's adoption of the idolizing song in the novel, *Vande Mataram* ('Praise to thee, Mother'), that caused dissent between the communities. Set in the backdrop of the famine of 1770, the novel depicts Hindu Bengali nationalism against the Muslim Nawab of Bengal, who is seen to be in collusion with the British.

Late 19th-century British India was also a time of rapid socio-economic change, and one in which the British had both racially retreated from and yet powerfully penetrated deeper into Indian society. British legal and constitutional laws began to permeate into wider society, while the British maintained their separate lives, in hill stations or cantonments. There were winners and losers; competition for resources was stiff, and increasingly a climate of widening communal tension between different religious communities took hold. By 1905, there was a widening rift between Hindus and Muslims on issues like language (Hindi vs Urdu) and cow slaughter, both of which caused major riots in the 1880s and 1890s. These issues contributed towards the decision of Viceroy Curzon to partition the province of Bengal into a Muslim majority east and a Hindu majority west. The administrative rationale offered for this partition was reversed in 1911, but by then the seeds of separation had sprouted. A rival to the Indian National Congress (INC; established 1885) had been formed, blessed by Curzon's successor Minto, to represent the disenchanted voices amongst the Muslim elite. The All-India Muslim League (AIML), formed in 1906, successfully negotiated with Minto for separate electorates in the newly expanded Legislative Councils under the 1909 Morley–Minto reforms. The separate electorates were reserved seats, in which only Muslims would be polled and elected. The idea, whilst protecting Muslim interests electorally and legislatively, entrenched the notion of a socially separate, minority community(-ies). Social and economic division was now firmly embedded in the political and constitutional framework, endorsed by the colonial power.

The Khilafat Movement (1919–23) temporarily brought together Indian nationalists in support of restoring the authority of the Ottoman caliphate following the end of the First World War. The Congress–League Lucknow Pact of 1916 saw a brief period in which the Congress agreed to the principle of separate electorates for Muslims in exchange for working towards full Indian autonomy. This collaboration, between the Congress and the League, between leading figures in the Khilafat movement, Begum Amman Bibi and her sons, Muhmmad and Shaukat Ali, and Mohandas Gandhi, was an alliance of convenience more than anything else. It however paved the way for a non-cooperation movement in the wake of the continued agitation following the massacre in Amritsar in 1919, in which General Dyer ordered troops to fire at an unarmed crowed enclosed in the gardens of Jallianwala Bagh, which resulted in the death of 379 people officially but many more unofficially. A fine reward for all the fighting that the Punjabis had done 'for King and another country', as Sharbani Basu explores in her book on Indian soldiers on the Western Front. Through these muddy waters emerged two figures who would dominate the politics of the subcontinent for the next thirty years: Gandhi and Jinnah, both Gujarati barristers by training, constitutionalists by temperament, and nationalists by character, who would eventually part ways and lead their people into two dominions, two destinies.

The Khilafat rug for Hindu–Muslim unity was anyway pulled from under its feet when Ataturk's Turkey abolished the caliphate in 1924. There now followed a decade of sharp deterioration in inter-faith relations, with some of the first, violent manifestations of communal rioting that would symbolize 1947. The inter-war period saw a gathering momentum behind the INC's mass freedom movement, simultaneous political devolution by the colonial state and persisting question marks, misgivings about the consequences of British departure and Congress (Hindu) rule across provinces, with the fear that Muslims (and not only them) would be relegated as the poor 'other'. Caste (Bhimrao Ramji Ambedkar), ethnicity (Erode Venkatappa Ramasamy), and class (Communist Party of India, established 1925) were all carved out as markers of separate spaces and opportunities in the political sphere, but none proved to be as powerful as religion.

The Pakistan Movement

Growing out of the landed gentry across north and east India, the League found its greatest inspiration in Sir Allama Mohammad Iqbal (1877–1938). Born in Sialkot to Kashmiri parents, educated in Lahore, Cambridge, and Munich and influenced by the poetry of Rumi, Iqbal put aside his academic and legal careers to write famous Urdu poems such as *Shikwa/Jawab-e-Shikwa* ('Complaint/Answer to the Complaint'). When elected as the AIML president in 1930, he delivered his aforementioned prophetic political speech on a 'Muslim India within India'. The 'formation of a consolidated North-West Indian Muslim State' appeared to him to be 'the final destiny of the Muslims of North-West India'.

Three years after this speech by the 'spiritual father of Pakistan', Choudhry Rahmat Ali (1897–1951), a young law student at the University of Cambridge, coined the term **PAKSTAN** (**P**unjab-Frontier (**A**fghan) Province-**K**ashmir-**S**indh-Balochist**an**) in his pamphlet, which was delivered to the delegates at the Third Round Table Conference in London in 1931–2 that was to consider the future government of India. These formulations would coalesce in Jinnah's address and the League's resolution at Lahore in 1940. The 'Lahore Resolution' became the linchpin of the 'Pakistan' movement, even though the word 'Pakistan' was not mentioned in it. Historians remain divided on how to interpret it, and for Ayesha Jalal this 'bargaining counter' did not irrevocably commit itself to the idea of a separation of land and transfer of population. Nevertheless, it became a decisive clarion call in the final cry for Muslim separate nationalism over 1946–7.

So, what had changed in those few short years? To begin with, the political climate in the provinces, with the coming of the Government of India Act 1935, which provided the constitutional blueprint for independent Pakistan till 1956. The franchise was expanded, and the system of diarchy furthered. In the 1936–7 elections, the INC performed well, winning across the board and leaving the AIML to wonder why it failed to connect with the Indian Muslims, especially where they were a majority population (in Punjab, Bengal, Sindh, NWFP, and Assam). In the two largest of these five provinces, Punjab and Bengal—which would go on to become the base of two independent nations, Pakistan in 1947 and Bangladesh, 1971—'regional' markers and class politics reigned in these inter-war years. However, the Congress rule from 1937 to 1939 in eight out of eleven provinces served to provide a taste of what a majoritarian state bureaucracy felt like, and thus gave a fillip to the League's efforts in the subsequent half-decade.

From 1939 to 1945, the events of the Second World War took over, wherein the Congress refused to cooperate with the British unless assured of independence immediately, while the League supported the war effort. A grateful colonial power seized upon this split and, while putting the entire Congress leadership behind bars for almost three years, promoted the League, thereby killing any possibility of a united nationalist movement. These years proved critical for the League's political prospects, as it won over the regional Muslim leaderships of the Punjab, from where 60 per cent of the soldiers of the British Indian army came by now, and which would be key in the Partition negotiations. By the winter of 1945–6, when another round of elections to central and provincial legislatures—sometimes called a referendum on Pakistan—were held, results confirmed this shift in opinion, as the AIML won all Muslim reserved seats in the central assembly, while forming the governments in Bengal and Sindh.

After tortuous negotiations over the prospects of a three-tier united India—Hindu provinces, Muslim provinces, and princely states—with a federal centre and constitution, the call for strength and thereby separation, immediate freedom and not protracted unity, proved too strong for the Congress, the League, and the by now desperate-to-decolonize British state. Ironically, the two regions/provinces to be partitioned were Punjab, which was again the province most involved in British war efforts, and Bengal, which had suffered the most because of these war efforts, which led to its famine of 1943–4. No side, however, could foresee that the progress towards political freedom would dissolve into the insanity of mayhem, migration, and mass murder witnessed in August 1947.

The Pakistan Movement's most rigorous historian, Ayesha Jalal, asked in the mid-1980s, how did a Pakistan come about that served the interests of so many Muslims of the subcontinent so little? Perhaps this was in response to the then-President General Zia-ul-Haq's pronouncement that if you took Islam out of Pakistan, it would collapse. But the question that pre-dates Jalal's is, how and why did the large Muslim populations of Punjab, Sindh, and Bengal—all between 50 per cent and 70 per cent— contribute so little and so late to specific and separate Muslim politics? Instead, at the forefront of Muslim politics were the so-called 'UP Muslims', a mere 14 per cent of the population of that province, but providing the road-map for Pakistan. This emergence of 'Muslim separatism'—real and imagined—in north India is a first-order fact to be grasped in any introduction to the present-day Pakistan.

In trying to theorize and understand this incongruence of people and politics, historian Francis Robinson's pioneering work on *Separatism Among Indian Muslims* is important. He examines four possibilities: first, Muslim backwardness since the mutiny of 1857, produced by British discrimination against them as a punishment for their part in the mutiny; second, British 'divide and rule' policy, breaking up the composite, syncretic subcontinental culture; third, Hindu revivalism in the garb of Indian nationalism, driving the Muslims to organize politically as a community; and finally, Indian Muslims as a separate entity since the days of Muhammad bin Qasim, with the creation of Pakistan an acknowledgement of this ever-present manifestation. That all these explanations share the assumption that 'Indian

Muslims were a group whose situation, outlook and interests were generally the same' should be noted, alongside the realization that this was not borne out in the behaviour of Balochis, Sindhis, Punjabis, Pashtuns, and Bengalis, who until almost the last stages were ambivalent about Muslim separatism.

The great irony of the Pakistan Movement is thus that the old Muslim centres such as Aligarh, Dacca (Dhaka), and Lucknow that were at the forefront of educational and organizational change are not in fact part of modern Pakistan. Moreover, Muslims that make up Pakistan today had organized their politics around non-communal lines, and the communal basis that it has held since 1947 emerged later. These incongruities and differing aspirations amongst the Muslims of India are borne out in many respects; Jinnah was no clearer than anyone else about what his new 'imagined homeland' would look like.

The creation of Pakistan was supposed to provide a single, peaceful political solution to the question of the self-determination of Muslims in British India. The reality was much more complex, because Muslims were scattered all over the eleven provinces of British India (Map 1) and were in a simple, numerical majority in only four of them. The rest—short of getting up and going to Pakistan—were to be locked in a deadly sacrificial relationship between a Hindu-majority India and a Muslim-saturated Pakistan. Not every Indian Muslim in the days leading up to independence wanted to be part of that separate political project. Indeed the 1951 census of Pakistan enumerates 7.2 million people as displaced persons (migrants from India); the majority located in West Pakistan. According to the 1951 census of India, 34 million or 10 per cent of the population were Muslims, indicating that more chose to remain than migrate. Furthermore, alongside British India, there existed over 550 princely states, semi-autonomous and indirectly ruled from Delhi, which comprised one-third of the land and a quarter of the population.

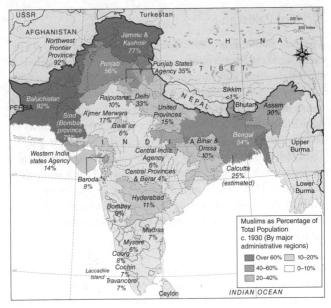

Map 1. Distribution of Muslim population in the subcontinent, *c*.1930.

They were theoretically independent when British paramountcy ended in 1947 but realistically had no chance of exercising that choice. Their integration in either of the independent dominions has been called a 'bloodless revolution' by historian Ian Copland, but it was a combination of bribery, chicanery, skulduggery with persuasion, coercion, and, in cases like Hyderabad, Junagadh and Jammu, and Kashmir, outright bloody annexation, leaving bitter legacies. The princely states that acceded to Pakistan, though smaller in number, were no less problematic, and accession and integration was a long-drawn-out affair, as historian Yaqoob Khan Bangash has detailed. Understanding contemporary conflicts in Balochistan also requires an appreciation of its history vis-à-vis the accession of the khanate of Kalat.

Birth of Pakistan

The final, frantic days of British rule saw Indian politicians at the helm in a short-lived coalition, the Interim Government, before the clouds parted and Partition appeared, with Mountbatten the last Viceroy. The fate of millions was decided by drawing a line on a map through the east and the west of the subcontinent, approximating to the Muslim-majority areas in western Punjab and eastern Bengal. Those caught in these widening communal cracks fell mercilessly. Pakistan was born out of this political end game, in which a colonial power wanted to avoid being embroiled in a long and bitter civil war and was looking for a quick exit, while the two main political parties were equally eager to grab their share of pie, as the only solution to the constitutional deadlock.

In his haste to leave, Mountbatten brought forward British departure from June 1948 to August 1947 and announced it on 3 June, leaving 72 days to undo a presence of 97 years in Punjab and 190 years in Bengal. The boundaries were drawn by the lawyer Cyril Radcliffe, flown in from the UK and asked to be swift, in the five weeks leading to British withdrawal. The boundary line was not made public until three days after the transfer of power at midnight on 14–15 August, for fear of people's response. This ill-conceived and ill-planned birth of Pakistan and independence of India created such a bitter-sweet moment that the trajectories of simultaneous celebrations and mourning can be traced to this day. For Pakistan this emergence was especially challenging, because not only was it a newly created nation-state, but everything had to be effectively set up from scratch. Moreover, while Jinnah achieved his life's calling, it was not quite the Pakistan he had expected. Instead, it was a Pakistan split into eastern and western wings, separated by 1,000 miles of what became hostile Indian territory. He would term it a 'mutilated, moth-eaten Pakistan'.

On 14 August 1947, Mohammad Ali Jinnah was in Karachi alongside Viceroy Mountbatten, welcoming a new dawn of freedom, engulfed in the fear and flames of communal violence. The worst of this occurred in the partitioned province of the Punjab in north India where, from March 1947 onwards, in Rawalpindi, communal violence and forced migration of people completely changed the landscape. Over the next year, but largely concentrated in August–December 1947, approximately 1 million people were massacred, and over 15 million were forced to leave from one side of the Radcliffe line to the other. Bengal in east India, the other province to be partitioned, experienced all this in slow motion, over almost twenty-five years. Other provinces in the newly created Pakistan, like Sindh and the NWFP, also saw religious riots and exchanges of refugee populations but remain dwarfed in this narrative, because the focus was dominated by the two borders of the new nations, cutting through two old regions.

The departing as well as the incoming authorities were unprepared for that moment when people would have to unceremoniously 'unmix' centuries of intermingling and living together. There was no blueprint for the migration of people who were forced to flee their homes due to the fear of violence that was spiralling out of control. This fear only highlighted the lack of preparedness of the authorities. The Partition and the momentous task of dealing with the refugee crisis was particularly acute in Pakistan, because in some areas the refugee population notably outnumbered the local population, with consequences for both. The unequal exchange of people affected Pakistan and India unequally and proved a bigger burden on the former's much smaller and more fragile state apparatus. Pakistan inherited a state that was structurally weak but with a strong military, and this would have implications in the years to come. But for now, it had to pick up the pieces and put together a new nation.

Chapter 4
Consolidation and fragmentation

Ever since Pakistan was created the pendulum for governing the country has swung between democracy and military rule on the one hand and secular state and religious state on the other. Was it a case of insufficient imagination? Or was it just unrealistic? For the democratically elected rulers, it has always been a case of holding onto power, given that the army has played and continues to play a crucial role behind the scenes. The consequence has been a weakening and erosion of institutional structures, party politics, and the public sphere, and conversely strengthening of the army. As is often said, nations have armies, but the Pakistani army has a nation. The strength of the army has been further consolidated by a civil bureaucracy of client–patron networks. Taken together, the army–bureaucracy nexus forms the cornerstone of Pakistan, as an Islamic nation-state. Some of this, such as the civil and military officialdom, is furniture inherited from the former colonial power; other aspects, such as the spreading tentacles of religious organizations, patronized and promoted, have grown in the postcolonial milieu.

The generals as saviours

In early 1949, Prime Minister Liaquat Ali Khan put forward the Objectives Resolution for Pakistan's new constitution, in which sovereignty first and foremost lay with Allah; a rather stunning

5. Liaquat Ali Khan, first prime minister of Pakistan (L) and
Mohammad Ali Jinnah (R).

about-turn from Jinnah's above-quoted words of mid-August 1947
(Figure 5). Seven years and four prime ministers later, the first
constitution was proclaimed in March 1956 and cemented
Pakistan's transformation from Jinnah's (undefined but secular)

vision to an Islamic republic. The passage of this time had less to do with drafting the clauses, many of which, as in neighbouring India, were borrowed from the Government of India Act 1935. It owed much more to the persisting political instability, especially since Liaquat was assassinated in October 1951. By October 1958, the government was taken over by a military coup, ushering in the first of four military dictators. In all, between them, the four generals-turned-presidents, Ayub Khan (1958–69), Yahya Khan (1969–71), Zia-ul-Haq (1977–88), and Pervez Musharraf (1999–2008), ruled Pakistan for almost thirty-five years, that is, half of its existence.

Even when not in power, the military has certainly controlled the strings in the background, never more so than in this last 'democratic decade' (2008–). These years of rule by technocrats, bureaucrats, and generals have all left an imprint on Pakistan, shaping and manipulating its identity to ensure that power and wealth remain concentrated in their hands. Another key feature is that whether it is Cold War politics, Islamization in the Zia period, or the 'war on terror' under Musharraf's regime, all served to ultimately strengthen the military establishment, and all have been endorsed by considerable US financial support. Indeed, when, in the late 1970s, the Jimmy Carter administration offered $400 million in assistance to Pakistan, Zia famously rejected this, calling the amount 'peanuts', and in the next decade helped funnel the Ronald Reagan administration's billion-plus dollars to the Afghan *mujahids* (religious warriors). Following the 'war on terror', aid to Pakistan increased eleven-fold to $2 billion in 2002, and the country became the third largest recipient of US military training and assistance during the Bush–Obama era. US aid to Pakistan has dramatically declined since the election of President Trump.

In 2013, for the first time, Pakistan transitioned formally from one elected government to another, breaking the pattern of alternating between elections and coups. Underneath this chronic instability was the fragmentation of the All-India Muslim League, as it sought to reinvent itself as the Pakistan Muslim League in 1947. The party struggled to transition from being the torchbearer of a movement to becoming the party of a government, in a regionalized, plural political set-up. Organizationally weak since its establishment by an elite in 1906, it was a party of landlords, aristocrats, businessmen, and intelligentsia but scarcely that of the peasant, the artisan, the trader, the worker, or the soldier. Its strong showing in Muslim constituencies in 1945–6 elections in a limited franchise counted for little in the post-1947 consolidation of the public sphere in Punjab, Bengal, Sindh, NWFP, and Balochistan—provinces where it had been a latecomer.

This, in turn, showed up its fragility and insecurity as it sought to adapt to the power sharing that was required in order to stabilize the partitioned provinces. The rot began at the top, where an ailing and old Jinnah assumed, unwisely perhaps, the unelected role of governor-general and president of the first Constituent Assembly. In doing so, he usurped the place of the elected role with a ceremonial role. In any case the Quaid-i-Azam died in September 1948, within thirteen months of Pakistan's formation, while his long-time deputy Liaquat was assassinated in public three years later. Thus, with the two founding fathers lost in its formative years, high politics in Pakistan resulted in what the historian Ian Talbot calls a game of 'musical chairs' at the top, played between the civil bureaucracy, military officials, and professional politicians against a backdrop of the developing Cold War and its pact-politics in the early 1950s.

Anxiety and lack of faith in democratic institutions was visible almost from the beginning. Jinnah had dismissed the chief minister of NWFP, Khan Abdul Jabbar Khan, popularly known as 'Dr Khan Sahib'. He was the elder brother of Khan Abdul Ghaffar Khan, famous as 'Frontier Gandhi' for his non-violent leadership of the anti-colonial resistance movement, Khudai Khidmatgars. Also known as Surkh Posh or the 'Red Shirts', they were a social reform organization that gradually turned to politics and, in coalition with the Congress, formed a ministry in NWFP in 1937 and 1946. They were staunchly against the Partition Plan, which the Congress accepted without consulting them, thus betraying the long-term association with the Khan brothers. The referendum in July 1947 in NWFP was supposed to end the anomaly of a Muslim majority province with a Congress government and provide the people with a say on whether they should join Pakistan. They voted in favour of Pakistan overwhelmingly, but it was boycotted by the Khudai Khidmatgar members. They were branded traitors and Indian sympathizers and punished by successive governments in Pakistan. Theirs was a poignant consequence of the peculiarity of partitioning a complex public sphere along a single axis: that of religion. Jinnah and the Muslim League showed an early intolerance for the Khan brothers and especially Ghaffar Khan, whose especial fraternal association with the Congress marked his anachronistic unsuitability for the emerging state narrative in Pakistan. He was imprisoned, his individuality and legacy ignored and erased from history books, and generations of Pakistanis have now grown up without any knowledge of that legendary figure and his anti-colonial movement in NWFP. Ghaffar Khan was cursed with a long life and only died in 1988, forty years after Jinnah and Gandhi.

His brother Dr Khan Sahib was not the only provincial premier dismissed by Jinnah though. The chief minister of Sindh, Muhammad Ayub Khuhro, was shown the door in April 1948. Khuhro had been concerned that the exodus of Hindu minorities from Sindh, complemented by the incoming *muhajirs* or refugees from different parts of India, would dilute the local Sindhi cultural identity. The reason for Khuhro's departure was his alleged corruption and misconduct, but in the case of Punjab's chief minister, Iftikhar Hussain Khan of Mamdot, there was nothing alleged about his 'unbelievably corrupt' regime, which ended in January 1949, when he chose to resign rather than face proceedings for his self-serving handling of the refugee rehabilitation and resettlement plans.

Collectively, these acts showed the thin emerging national layer overarching these regional spaces and undermined the fledgling politicians and fragile democratic structures; instead, they strengthened the military, the bureaucracy/technocracy, and the religious establishment. Successive military dictators have depicted the politicians as capricious, corrupt, and motivated by self-interest, while projecting themselves as saviours of the nation. The ease of their success confirms the grain of genuineness in the charge but that often came with setting the country's constitutional clock back to colonial-era laws and their preference for strong and centralized power levers. In the six years from the assassination of Liaquat, Pakistan saw six prime ministers, and by the summer of 1958, Defence Secretary-turned-President Iskander Mirza and his successor, General Ayub Khan, had separately telegraphed their intentions towards and preferences for a dictatorship to the American ambassador, then as until recently Pakistan's most valuable diplomatic relationship.

While the general at-the-top functioned as a suitable public face, underneath a strong military establishment emerged, which spread its tentacles into numerous areas and key components of the economy. The *Fauji* Foundation was established in 1954 to provide employment and welfare benefits to ex-military personnel. Today, its cradle-to-grave character is clear from its involvement in items as disparate as cereals, gas, cement, oil, meats, fertilizer, and wind energy, to name a few. The Askari Bank (established 1991), the Army Welfare Trust (established 1971), the Evacuee Trust Property Board (established 1960), and the Defence Housing Authority, operating in the major cities and often located in the wealthiest parts, all feed into a wider economy of the military–industrial complex. Ayesha Siddiqa's *Military Inc.* (2007) provides an in-depth analysis of an elaborate system by which the military and its secret services operate and control vast swathes of Pakistan's economy. The military institution is intuitively invested in sustaining and maintaining itself by keeping an external threat (which is often India) alive, and which Ayesha Jalal termed the political economy of defence.

Cosmopolitan Karachi

Although the majority of the partition-related disturbances, murders, and migration in 1947–8 happened in Punjab, and a little later in 1949–50 (and beyond) for Bengal, the magnet for Muslim migrants from north India was Pakistan's first capital, Karachi (Figure 6). The quiet 18th-century pier and the quaint 19th-century metropolis located on international seaways and airways now underwent a total transformation. This one-time fishing village, at the mouth of the Indus, had come into prominence following the annexation of Sindh by the British East India Company in 1843. By the time Jinnah was born there in 1876, Karachi was a thriving commercial cosmopolitan port-city, boasting one of the first tramway systems in South Asia. Opened by 1885, it only stopped operating in 1975.

6. The Teen Talwar (Three Swords) monument in Karachi is inscribed with Unity, Faith, and Discipline. Commissioned by PM Bhutto in 1973.

The two world wars saw the city's strategic value soar. By now, it was the capital of the youngest British Indian province of Sindh and its local levers of political power and economic affluence were in the hands of Sindhi Hindus, even though as a whole its demography was majority Muslim. Above all, it nursed and cherished a Sindhi regional and linguistic identity that equally resisted Punjab's dominance in emerging Pakistan as well as resented the incoming *muhajirs*. These millions of refugees, who had made the ideological and existential journey of mind and body, were received with a sullen ambivalence at best, and open hostility at worst—neither commensurate with their sacrifice nor with the expectations set in motion by the Pakistan Movement.

A considerable and sensitive strand in the Partition literature shows the tragic refugee sacrifice (*muhajir qurbani*) in Karachi and across Sindh. The entitlements felt by one group (north Indian Muslims) clashed with the expectations of another (local Sindhi Muslims); while the former had been at the forefront of the Pakistan Movement from the beginning, the latter had shored up its spine in the end. Whose was the greater sacrifice for a homeland? Surely those who ultimately left, or were driven away from, their ancestral homes and flocked to this new Medina? Arrival was not easily followed by assimilation and, over the years, the local political conflict of Karachi coalesced around the *muhajir* fault-line, as their demographic impact was substantial. In 1941, the population of Karachi had been 435,000. Ten years later, the numbers had soared to over 1 million, of which the *muhajirs* comprised 55 per cent, thereby making the local Sindhis a minority. Ultimately, in the twenty years between 1941 and 1961, Karachi's population grew by an astounding 432 per cent, a staggering rate of growth which, as the geographer Oskar Spate exclaims, no other city anywhere else in the world at any time in human history has ever experienced.

The fallout of this astounding growth was a heightened sense of regionalism in the 1950s, a decline in 'national' politics in the

1960s, and labour unrest in the 1970s. By then, the *muhajirs* had also organized, with the establishment of the All Pakistan Muhajir Student Organization, founded in 1978. It was the precursor to the Muhajir Qaumi Movement (renamed Muttahida Qaumi Movement—MQM in 1984), which was founded by Altaf Hussain to protect the rights of *muhajirs* from a quota system that would reduce their access to opportunities, and argued that the *muhajirs* constituted the fifth ethnic group in Pakistan. The MQM dominated the political landscape in Karachi from 1988, thanks to the successful mobilization of ethnic nationalism and militancy. This prompted the government of Pakistan in 1992 to send the military to Karachi to 'cleanse' the city of 'anti-social' elements, namely the MQM. Hussain fled to the UK, where he sought and received political asylum, but he continued with his political ambitions despite being implicated in the murder of a senior party member, Imran Farooq, in 2010. In August 2016, speaking from his north London base, Hussain lambasted Pakistan as a 'cancer for the entire world' and the 'epicentre of terrorism'. This call to incite his supporters into action led to horrific violence in Karachi, and despite the apology by Hussain a few days later, Farooq Sattar broke rank and the party split in 2017, with MQM-P operating from Pakistan, and Hussain controlling the MQM-London party.

The MQM's political growth coincided with and contributed to a period of immense political instability and violence in the city of Karachi. The late 1980s and especially the 1990s reduced Karachi to one of the most dangerous cities in the world, whose 'ordered disorder' only began to stabilize following the military crackdown in 2013. Through these decades, it served as a destination for refugees fleeing the war(s) in Afghanistan and was flooded by the flotsam and jetsam of American weaponry meant for the *mujahids* in Afghanistan. The wider, longer-term consequences of this were a society saturated with firearms and embroiled in drug trafficking and extortionist activities, real estate mafias, and politics by violence, giving rise to the term 'Kalashnikov Culture'. In 2016 Amjad Sabri, a popular *qawwali* (Sufi devotional song) singer, was shot dead in Karachi. He was targeted as a consequence of being caught up in the widespread violence, political and general, that has cursed the city. While the murder was widely condemned, it highlighted how deep the rot had penetrated.

For Karachi to become the dual capital of Pakistan and the province of Sindh was not inevitable. Multan was in the running because it was located in the heart of Pakistan and, as seen previously, was an established, holier, and more historic city. There was some support for Dhaka in East Pakistan, but it had been peripheral in the Pakistan Movement and, although a strong contender, Lahore was unfortunately badly affected by the chaos and violence following Partition. Also, it was too close to the newly created border with India. Karachi, on the other hand, was relatively far away and calm. It offered opportunities to be connected to the outside world via sea and air and had an existing infrastructure which could be expanded. Thus, Jinnah and Liaquat Ali Khan leapt at the chance of turning Karachi into the capital of the new nation, when the Sindh Muslim League offered. In turn, Hyderabad now became the regional capital of Sindh.

This arrangement proved short-lived and by 1959 Ayub Khan had announced that the capital would be shifted to the garrison city of Rawalpindi, while a twin city would be built nearby. It was a bold and dramatic move, and while Ayub found the tropical climate of Karachi unfavourable, moving the capital to the more sedate climate of the Margalla Hills also allowed the military general headquarters (GHQ) to converge and converse closely with the new political capital: Islamabad. This 'city of Islam' was designed by the Greek architect C. A. Doxiadis and funded by international organizations such as the Ford Foundation in America. It was a purpose-built planned city that encapsulated the era of Khan's modernist vision for Pakistan, which was to be realized under the watchful eyes of the nearby military GHQ. This shift also finalized the break with the declining old guard of the pre-1947 Muslim

League politics and crowned the domination of Punjabis and Pashtuns in the new political-bureaucratic-military nexus. Modern Karachi is politically peripheral but remains at the core of commerce, trade, and cultural activities, a cosmopolitan melting pot of hope and aspiration for many who continue to flock to this great metropolis on the shores of the Arabian Sea.

Bangladesh breaks away

Although Pakistan was imagined as a homeland for the Muslims of India, it was never a wholly Muslim country, nor did it encompass all Indian Muslims. Its 1951 census had yielded a combined population of 76 million, of which the majority, 42 million, lived in East Pakistan (Bengal). Almost 23 per cent of this population were Bengali Hindus, while by contrast West Pakistan only had a minority population of 3 per cent. Although a greater number of Hindus initially remained in the eastern wing, by 1950–1 it became clear that the upper- and middle-class Hindu *bhadralok* (genteel) preferred to migrate to India. This in turn created openings in the administrative services for educated Muslims in eastern India, who were attracted to Dhaka, the new-old capital of East Pakistan. Back in 1905, the division of British India's Bengal province had set a precedent for Dhaka's elevation as the provincial capital of the eastern part, a status which it soon lost when this partition was annulled in 1911. Now in the early 1950s, although sharing the same faith, the two wings of Pakistan were unable to bridge the physical and the otherwise quite distinct, linguistic, ethnic, cultural, climatic, and historical differences.

From the beginning, then, Pakistan was faced with the challenges of first trying to keep two physically separate wings connected, and second trying to construct a national 'Muslim' identity from a population that was otherwise fragmented along linguistic, cultural, ethnic, and economic lines. United Province's Urdu-speaking elite, who had come to have close ties with the political establishment in Karachi upon their migration and shared its attachment to a one-nation, one-culture, one-language policy, propelled the Constituent Assembly's rejection of Bangla/Bengali as a state language, and its refusal to hold sessions in Dhaka. This was the trigger for Bengali alienation from Pakistan, which grew through the 1950s and to which other grievances, principally economic, became added. It would test the limits of the two-nation theory to its core, as the question persisted: was Islam sufficient to keep the two wings together?

In March 1948, against the background of rising agitation against this imposition of Urdu, Jinnah made his first and last trip to the eastern side of the country. Addressing an audience of half a million people at the Ramna Racecourse Maidan, Dacca (Dhaka), he acknowledged the importance of east Bengal and how efforts were being made to ensure that East Pakistan 'attains its full stature with the maximum speed'. He claimed that Pakistan, overall, had done much to ensure that minorities were protected during these difficult times, despite evidence to the contrary. His speech reflected the early anxiety and insecurity felt by the fragile state, with references to 'enemies of the state, subversive elements, communists and fifth columnists', all conspiring to divide and destroy this new homeland. But, above all, to the crowd's disbelief, the speech, delivered in English and addressed to a Bengali audience, reaffirmed Urdu as the state language.

Urdu, of course, was not just a lingua franca; it was symbolically and ideologically attached to the Pakistan Movement. For a singular national identity to emerge, the political leadership felt that there should be one national language, but the reality on the ground was that this flowery language of poetry and pathos, written in flowing Persian calligraphy, was only spoken by the small elite from the United Provinces (now the ruling class and based in Karachi), who had imagined and articulated this project. The protests were swift. Civic unrest escalated and, by 1952, the Urdu–Bengali controversy was at boiling point, despite the ascent of a Bengali governor-general, Khawaja Nazimuddin, for the whole of Pakistan, as Jinnah's successor. Nazimuddin, despite being Bengali, inflamed the language debate by defending the Urdu-only policy. Maulana Bhashani, co-founder of the Muslim Awami League (established 1949), warned the West Pakistani leadership against the imposition of Urdu and was already demanding independence.

The 'unlawful assembly' of demonstrators under Section 144, centred around the University of Dhaka, ended in confrontations with the police on 21 February 1952. Over the next few days, the demonstrators grew to thousands, with the authorities using tear gas and firing to suppress the young student protesters. Officially, five martyrs are commemorated on this day, unofficially the numbers were most likely higher. The government blamed Hindus, communists, and others plotting against the state, rather than rectifying the genuine grievances. Since the year 2000, in recognition of these events, 21 February is observed by the United Nations as the International Mother Language day to highlight and celebrate linguistic diversity. The intensity of these language riots showed up the interregional and intra-communal fault-line in Pakistan's early demographic composition. It dwarfed in symbolism and long-term significance the Liaquat–Nehru Pact of 1950 signed between India and Pakistan, with a mutually reinforcing aim to protect the rights of religious minorities in their midst. It reflected the genuine concerns that the Bengalis (Hindus and Muslims) harboured about becoming the inferior 'other' in Pakistan, starting with losing state recognition and patronage of their proud, regional vernacular, captured by prolific writers such as Shamsur Rahman and Kazi Nazrul Islam, who became the national poet of Bangladesh.

In 1954, the One Unit programme was launched by PM Muhammad Ali Bogra, becoming implemented by PM Chaudhri Muhammad Ali on 14 October 1955 (Figure 7). The programme significantly sought to merge the four provinces of the western wing to outmatch East Pakistan for administrative purposes. In 1954 elections took place in East Pakistan, in which the Muslim League

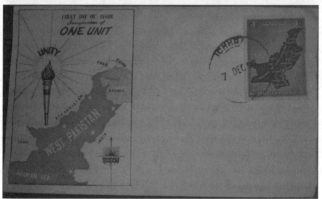

7. **Postcards commemorating the One Unit Scheme, 1955.**

was defeated at the hands of the United Front led by the former prime minister of Bengal, A. K. Fazlul Huq's Krishak Sramik Party (Farmer–Labour Party) and Maulana Bhashani's Awami League. It would turn out to be a turbulent year in the trajectory of united Pakistan, with industrial unrest and labour riots in the east, blamed upon 'enemy agents' by the west-based central government, which imposed direct rule. This authoritarian attitude of Karachi towards Dhaka set the template for future transactions until the 'unmaking' of this united Pakistan, fifteen years later.

With the creation of the 'One Unit' to counter East Pakistan, issues of domination and representation only became starker, even as, in 1956, Karachi relented and gave Bengali official recognition. By then, the physical separation and emotional distance between the two wings were becoming worse through growing economic disparity, which would culminate in a conflict over state sovereignty and the very meaning of 'nationhood'. Soon, insult was to be added to this injury by Ayub Khan and his military ilk, who were quasi-racist in their scathing dismissal of the east Bengalis, formerly under subjugation until Pakistan was created, and regarded as still under the influence of an 'effeminate' Hindu culture and language. Hence their reluctance to embrace a more 'martial' Islamic identity, as evident in the western wing.

The arrogance and prejudice, disdain and discrimination for the eastern province was not just visible in the racialized language used but was starkly apparent in who was controlling the purse strings, and the narrative around national identity. For many, East Pakistan was merely a colony. The western province dominated the political, bureaucratic, and military class, while much of the economy in the early days was heavily dependent on the jute exports from the eastern side. One of the largest jute-processing factories in the world was located in the suburbs of Dhaka but was owned by the Adamjee family in the western wing. Insofar as investment, infrastructure, and welfare went, there was a stark indifference to East Pakistan, neglect, and what amounted almost to neo-colonialism. Between 1950 and 1970, the ratio of government spending between west and east wings was estimated to be 70:30. In 1966, the Bengali politicians put together a six-point programme seeking a federal constitution, convertible currencies, power to tax and spend, separate foreign exchange reserve, and separate paramilitary forces, especially navy—given the long coastline in the east. Drafted, amongst others, by Rehman Sobhan and Nural Islam, the proposal for greater provincial autonomy was rejected by politicians in West Pakistan and those not aligned to the Awami League. The disparity between the two wings was evident in the military administrator's response, when the deadly Bhola cyclone ravaged the southern districts of East Pakistan on 12 November 1970, killing an estimated 300,000–500,000 people. The failure to respond with immediacy, declaring a national emergency, and the lack of adequate relief, only confirmed the wider feelings of neglect and exploitation felt in the eastern wing.

Under the clouds of growing instability, following transition from one military dictator to another, the first national elections took place in December 1970. They were scheduled to take place on 5 October but were postponed due to floods. The results showed a resounding victory for the East Pakistan-based Awami League and its leader Sheikh Mujibur Rahman. The party fought on the Six-Points programme, and won 160 out of the 300 seats, representing 39 per cent of the popular vote. However, the West Pakistan-based Pakistan Peoples Party, led by Zulfikar Ali Bhutto, which won 81 seats, refused to recognize these results. The incumbent regime of General Yahya Khan attempted to foster an agreement between the two parties, even as the situation on the ground was deteriorating towards a civil war. Attempting to project the army as the saviour once again, Operation Searchlight began from March 1971, under the pretext of checking outbreaks of anti-Bihari violence by east Bengalis.

Over the summer of 1971, the Pakistan army systematically targeted pro-independence supporters in Dhaka and the Bengal countryside, killing a generation of students, academics, workers, committing mass rapes against women, atrocities against minorities, and leaving deep scars across a region and soon to be a nation. Typically, there can be little agreement on how many died, with the Bangladeshis putting this figure at 3 million. As ever, the real brunt of the brutality unleashed that year, told through women's testimonies—the silent sufferers in this human tragedy—is being narrated only now, the 50th year of Bangladesh's birth. By the monsoon-autumn of 1971, approximately 9 million refugees had fled across the border into India and, with consequent Indian intervention, the year ended in the third India–Pakistan war that culminated in the creation of Bangladesh in December 1971. As the political commentator Tariq Ali remarks, 'the "two-nation" theory, formulated in the middle-class living rooms of Uttar Pradesh, was buried in the Bengali countryside'. The bloody stains of this 'spectral wound' and brutal genocide have left an indelible mark on the subcontinent, and Bangladesh was in many ways the definitive 'unfinished business of Partition'. It would take until February 1974 for the 90,000 Pakistani prisoners of war to return home and Pakistan to give diplomatic recognition to Bangladesh. This came on an occasion which portended the Islamic turn that the country would take, as PM Bhutto received and fêted Sheikh Mujib, along with thirty-six other heads of state from among the major Muslim nations of the world in Lahore that month. Addressing a packed Lahore television studio, a visibly emotional Bhutto declared in Urdu, 'In the name of Allah and on behalf of the peoples of this country, I declare that we are recognizing Bangladesh.'

In retrospect, perhaps it was inconceivable that two such disparate provinces could exist as one country, despite the technological advances made in the 20th century, without a true spirit of accommodation and power-sharing. From that viewpoint, it is in fact remarkable that they managed to do so for almost twenty-five years. Although Pakistan began from an institutionally weak position, it was this break-up of the two wings that led (formerly West) Pakistan towards a path not envisioned by the Quaid-i-Azam. Pakistan now entered a new Islamic phase of its history, armed with another constitution (1973), to meet another existential crisis. Rather than embrace and celebrate diversity, under the elected Bhutto and the dictator General Zia ul-Haq, the regime once again opted for the opposite. Its aim now was for a totally homogeneous Islamic identity around its majority Sunni faith, Persianized Urdu, and Arabified idioms.

Chapter 5
Building the land of the pure

Under the first fully elected, albeit belatedly formed, government of by-now halved Pakistan, PM Zulfikar Ali Bhutto turned to the religious clergy for support and the new constitution of the newly christened 'Islamic Republic'. Looking back, this move marks the slow but sure shift towards political orthodoxy in Pakistan in line with the increasing influence of the Sunni state of Saudi Arabia. Excluding and reaffirming the religious identity of Pakistan has been at the core of building the land of the pure, but the voices of dissent to this one way of imagining a nation have also persisted. That this land of plenty, striking in its contradictions, persists is due to the singular thread of the 'idea of Pakistan', whose 'sole spokesman' kept it going, and whose sole shadow keeps its realization going. Building sturdy blocks from this rather thin thread, though, has been more challenging and highlights the fragility of the state.

Excluding and reaffirming

Ironically, the road towards overt religious nationalism had not been enough for one of the leading groups of Islamic scholars (*ulema*), the Jamaat-e-Islami (JI), which had, to begin with, been opposed to the idea of a territorially bound Muslim homeland at all, favouring a more wide-reaching pan-Islamic community or *ummah*. Founded in 1941 by Syed Abul A'la Maududi, a journalist by training, in response to the 1940 'Lahore Resolution' that he considered un-Islamic, the JI soon went on to spearhead the movement towards creating a theocratic state in Pakistan. As early as the early 1950s, it was at the forefront of a campaign against the Ahmadiyya community, demanding that the state declare them non-Muslims, resulting in rioting and the imposition of martial law in Lahore in 1953. Despite being imprisoned, Maududi and supporters of the JI retained their influence and saw the spirit behind some of their demands percolate through the letters of the 1956 constitution.

Although not a major electoral player, the JI has fielded its candidates in polls. Maududi grudgingly supported the candidacy of Fatima Jinnah (sister of Jinnah) in the 1965 presidential election, despite his aversion to a female being head of state in a Muslim country. However, under the devout Zia, the JI found the space to spread and that, in turn, provided the ideological foundations for the general's Islamization. Zia personally received his Islamic inspiration from the Deobandi movement that had developed in British India. This was growing in popularity as the medieval and early modern Perso-Turkish-Afghan influences gradually diminished, making way for the bankrolled Saudi brand of modern and more puritanical Sunni Islam. Maududi had nurtured a close relationship with the royal House of Saud. In 1981, the bond between religion and nation was further reinforced and institutionalized. *Nazriya-e-Pakistan* (the ideology of Pakistan), which equated Pakistan with Islam, was now taught to all students.

However, opportunism and division along sectarian lines have also continued. The populist pulls of religion, moral and social, remain prominent but are also fragmented. Both Bhutto and Zia fraternized with religious parties and if it was the sterner vein of Islam coming from Saudi Arabia that took root in Pakistan, that was in the wake of wider global concerns around the Iranian Revolution and the Soviet invasion of Afghanistan in 1979. Several factors converged in the 1970s–1980s. With East Pakistan becoming Bangladesh, the growing Pakistani diaspora in the gulf's globalizing economy became couriers for Saudi influence, while remitting its excess petro-dollars. Investments in *madrassa* (religious school) education, mosques, and other institutions in Pakistan cemented this shift towards pious conservatism. There was an exponential increase in the number of new madrassas; between 1979 and 1982 approximately 151 new madrassas had been built, but from 1982 to 1987, nearly 1,000 more opened. The majority of these were Sunni and followed the Deobandi sect.

The mercurial and enigmatic Zulfikar Ali Bhutto was a political leader who changed the appearance and articulation of the masculine public sphere by popularizing the traditional *shalwar kameez* among the elites and the masses alike and by bringing in the rhetoric of Islamic socialism through his Pakistan People's Party (established 1967). Feeling the need to inject a strong sense of an Islamic national pride after the defeat to India and the loss of east Bengal, Bhutto embarked upon a nuclear programme for Pakistan in 1972. He had famously said that 'if India builds the bomb, we will eat grass or leaves, even go hungry, but we will get one ... we have no alternative'. Zia, on the other hand, changed the way people read, wrote, and, eventually, how they thought, especially at the grass roots, among the rural countryside, and away from the urban Anglicized elite and middle classes. Within a generation, the young population across Pakistan, notwithstanding pockets of affluence and outside (global) influences, was drifting away from traditional feudal politics and embracing the new populisms of global capital and global Islam. This transformation became complete with the rise of Imran Khan Niazi, the superstar cricketer and playboy turned religious patriarch, the face of this new Pakistan and its prime minister since 2018.

America's 'war on terror' since 2001 proved to be a particularly polarizing time for Pakistan. There has been a substantial increase

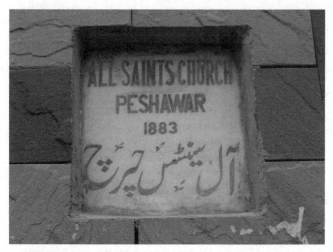

8. All Saints' Church, inside Kohati Gate, Walled City of Peshawar. A suicide attack outside the church in 2013 killed 127 people.

in internal violence and terrorism and the country has paid heavily in casualties (Figure 8). Before 2001, suicide bombings were virtually unknown in Pakistan; by 2009 there had been seventy-six suicide attacks and countless fatalities. A combination of poor governance, external geopolitical agendas, mismanagement of the economy, hyper-nationalism/militarism, increased irrational religiosity, all coupled with old-fashioned personal rivalries has created a toxic environment in which political violence thrives. Pakistan is, at its core, a conservative, traditional, and religious society, but not necessarily a theocratic state. Certainly, as a society Pakistan has become more self-consciously religious compared to the secular ideals proposed by Jinnah in the first year after its creation.

By the mid-1970s, the 'core' of Islamic values of this society became visible in the state's consolidation of a national identity. In doing so, the question of who is a Pakistani became central and, moreover, increasingly exclusionary. Acquiring a Pakistan passport is a prime example of this, a process which requires declaring Mirza Ghulam Ahmad (1835–1908) and his followers, the Ahmadis, as impostors. The group was declared to be non-Muslim by Bhutto in 1974. He took the first steps towards turning Pakistan into a Sunni majoritarian country, which was further consolidated into law and society by Zia. This institutionalized discrimination compels Ahmadis to declare themselves as non-Muslim (though they would self-identify as Muslim), in order to access rights accorded to other citizens.

Since 1974, targeting of the Ahmadiyya community has gradually increased, and in 2010 there was a major attack by the Tehrik-e-Taliban group on two Ahmadi mosques in Lahore, in which ninety-four people died. Sir Muhammad Zafarullah Khan, a legal luminary who served as Pakistan's first foreign minister (1947–54) and rose to become the president of the International Court of Justice (1970–3), was an Ahmadi, as was Abdus Salam, Pakistan's first Nobel Prize winner for Physics (1979). Both have been virtually erased from the history books. Buried in the Pakistani town of Rabwah, a major centre for Ahmadis, Salam's tombstone was desecrated in 2010, when the word 'Muslim' was painted over in the inscription that called him 'the first Muslim Nobel laureate'. In Pakistan today, the numbers of the Ahmadiyya community are estimated to be around 1–3 million, and the existential question they face, ironically, remains true for most of Pakistan too, that is, who is a Pakistani?

Other minorities are targeted with the use of blasphemy laws, a crime punishable by death. One of the most shocking attacks recently was in 2017, when the victim was a young student. Mashal Khan was an aspiring Pashtun student of journalism at Abdul Wali Khan University in Mardan, KP, when he was dragged out of his room in the university hostel by a crowd of students, beaten, and shot dead, with graphic images of his defiled body shared widely on social media. Just 23 years old, Mashal Khan had, earlier in the day, been accused of posting blasphemous content online, though the fact that he had made allegations of corruption against some university staff may have been more pertinent. He had been open and vocal about sharing his liberal secular views and was seen as a 'threat' that had to be put down, brutally.

In another prominent case, Asia Bibi, a Christian woman, was convicted of blasphemy and sentenced to death in 2010. She was eventually acquitted in a high-profile case in 2018 due to insufficient evidence, but it was impossible for her to remain in Pakistan, because of the death threats against her and her family. Huge protests erupted following the acquittal, forcing her into hiding before eventually claiming asylum in France. That the threat to her life was not imaginary had been highlighted by the assassinations in 2011 of figures such as Salman Taseer, the then governor of Punjab, and Shahbaz Bhatti, a federal minister for minorities, for their opposition to the blasphemy laws and for supporting Asia Bibi. Taseer's convicted killer, Mumtaz Qadri, instead of being vilified, became something a celebrity in Pakistan. The funeral following his execution in 2016 drew hundreds of thousands of people in a brazen public display of hero worship. Qadri's execution was also a catalyst for the rise of the right-wing Islamist party, the Tehreek-e-Labbaik Pakistan.

Historically, the British-era laws around blasphemy had been designed to prosecute faith leaders, writers, or those promoting intercommunal violence. They are now openly used to charge and accuse people of blasphemy. The statistics around the use/abuse of this law are startling. Before 1986, only 14 cases were reported under these laws; however, between 1987 and 2017 the figure jumped dramatically, to 1,472 people. Mainstream parties have been reluctant to speak up in support of repealing these laws because of their fear of Islamic parties and an Islamized public they have helped create over the years. Those individuals who dare to do so risk their lives.

During this process of defining Pakistan, the idea of who was a legitimate and worthy citizen increasingly became, and has remained, prescriptive and exclusionary. This set the foundations for a double 'othering' within the country: first, of the non-Muslims, and second, of the 'bad' Muslims. This is most stark in the Arabization of Pakistan's culture, spiritual space, idioms, and religious-economic ties towards Mecca/Medina. The medieval eastward movement of Islam, which enriched it in Persia, Central Asia, and South Asia, now stands not merely downplayed but turned back fully in terms of its historical and cultural imaginations.

Civil society as survivors

Forming the counterpart to any functioning state, democratic or not, is a strong civil society which has the capacity to speak freely. With no elections from a universal franchise in its first twenty-three years, twelve of which were spent under martial law, concepts like 'public sphere', 'civil society', and 'free press' become relative in Pakistan. But as is often the way, overt state oppression presents opportunities for covert resistance by groups that mobilize underground. One problem in Pakistan from the outset was that the urban middle class was and remains a smaller group when compared with the numbers in provincial towns and the rural countryside. Those above it form a tight-knit, well-networked elite, while those below comprise the masses, among whom a third are still counted as illiterate, with great variation between regions and by gender. Rallying them together behind the difficult and what must appear as 'foreign' concept of 'freedoms' or 'human rights' has been a concern for many of the country's activist movements. Lawyers, journalists, women's rights groups, student organizations, artists, and academics have often been at the heart of such movements and have played an important part in offering an opposition, when democratic institutions have been rendered irrelevant.

The decline in democratic values set in under Jinnah, who, as noted above, himself set precedents of meeting dissent with dismissal. Liaquat followed in earnest by concentrating power at the centre and playing off the bickering provincial elite. Faiz Ahmed Faiz, who had been editor of *The Pakistan Times* from before independence, was imprisoned in early 1951 in the notorious Rawalpindi Conspiracy Case, an alleged *coup d'état* against Liaquat's government led by Major General Akbar Khan. Later that year, Liaquat himself was sensationally gunned down in circumstances that remain unresolved to this day. The whole chain of events provided a cue to rid the public sphere of intellectuals like Faiz and political activists like Sajjad Zaheer, the first secretary of the Communist Party of Pakistan.

The Communist Party of Pakistan was eventually banned in 1954, making clear the state's lack of tolerance for critical voices, particularly on the left, and never had the chance to grow into a mass movement, in spite of its influence in neighbouring USSR and China and presence in India. Peasant or *kisan* movements, despite their existence, have been unsuccessful in enforcing land reform, and thus power and wealth remain concentrated in the hands of a few. Refuting the claims by Ayub Khan of a 'decade of development', the Chief Economist of the Planning Commission in 1968 identified Pakistan's twenty-two richest families, which collectively owned 87 per cent of the banking and insurance industry and controlled 66 per cent of the industries. Although the number of families has expanded and grown, wealth (and power) is still woefully concentrated. Even the charismatic Bhutto and his populist 'Islamic Socialism' around the dreams of '*roti, kapda aur makan*' ('food, clothing, and shelter'), which promised much in the form of redistribution of wealth and nationalization of key industries, failed to break the power of a feudal system and elitism in Pakistani society, of which he was himself a part.

Over the years, though, some movements, or more accurately 'moments', have managed to challenge state power. Jinnah's sister,

Fatima Jinnah, became the figurehead of a movement to restore democracy in 1968, consisting of students, workers, writers, and lawyers that provided the critical mass, forcing Ayub to step aside in late 1969, in that time of worldwide protests. A variation of this activism was seen twelve years later under Zia, with the establishment of the Women's Action Forum in 1981. And, in 2007, it was the lawyers' movement, or the Movement for the Restoration of Judiciary, which erupted when Musharraf unconstitutionally suspended the chief justice of the supreme court. This morphed into a broader agitation against Musharraf, leading to his departure the next year. Another trigger for this protest movement was the complicity of intelligence agencies in hundreds of cases of 'missing persons', without due investigation. 'Black Coats' filled the streets in a 'Long March' and, for a brief moment, the lawyers' movement became more than just about reinstating the chief justice. Unfortunately, though not unsurprisingly, once the individual was reinstated in 2009, the broader range of grievances of the movement lost traction.

The strong presence of the army in the public sphere, with the consequent infringement of freedom of speech and association, has continued to both make and mar student politics and youth movements from the 1950s. Most recently, Manzoor Ahmad Pashteen, a young and charismatic human rights activist from South Waziristan, received considerable support in his endeavours to raise awareness around the plight of the Pashtun people, especially in the FATA areas, which have remained highly militarized as a key battleground in the ongoing 'war on terror'. The Pashtun Tahafuz Movement began with a march from Dera Ismail Khan, KP in January 2018. By the time it reached Islamabad (approx. 350 km), it had also gained the support and sympathy of broader pro-democracy groups. The usual allegations of Pashteen being a 'foreign agent' circulated, followed by charges under the colonial-era sedition laws, which are often used to criminalize political dissent. Criticism of the military is still rare and underlying the movement have been the increasing disappearances of people critical of the establishment and those investigating these cases. Coverage of the rallies is strictly censored, and any hint of support is suspicious.

Resistance by women

Buried beneath the masculinized stock-phrases and images of the military, the terrorist, and the fundamentalist on the one hand and stereotypes of burqa-clad women on the other, which saturate much international media, there is a strain of history in Pakistan that is seldom discussed. At key junctures, women have been both a catalyst as well as carriers of the voice and mood of the nation. Among the female participants in the Pakistan Movement, Ra'ana Liaquat Ali Khan, wife of the former prime minister, and Shaista Suhrawardy Ikramullah, wife of the first foreign secretary of Pakistan, used their privilege to promote women's participation in national activities, to contribute socially and economically, especially in refugee relief and rehabilitation following Partition.

They had been inspired by Jinnah, who in his speech of March 1940 had voiced his belief that it was 'absolutely essential for us to give every opportunity to our women to participate in our struggle of life and death...because if political consciousness is awakened amongst our women, remember your children will not have much to worry about'. Subsequently, in 1949, Ra'ana played a key role in establishing the All Pakistan Women's Association, which worked towards better education for girls and cultural uplifting of women. Shaista became a diplomat and ensured that at least some women, even if from middle-upper classes, were visible in public spaces in these early years.

Above and beyond them stood the figure of Fatima Jinnah, trained as a dental surgeon in the 1920s and a stalwart figure alongside her brother. Following his death, she was forced to withdraw from public life, until she returned for a swansong in the 1965 presidential election as a strong, sentimental, and nostalgic opponent against

General Ayub Khan. She was the figurehead for the Combined Opposition Parties and tried to capitalize on her brother's name, but the elections were widely believed to be rigged and there was little chance of her succeeding. She died two years later but left behind a legacy, recently resurrected, as 'mother of the nation'.

Twenty years later, women again emerged as the strongest opponents of yet another general-turned-president, Zia-ul-Haq. In 1985, the noted singer Iqbal Bano defied a ban on the *sari* (now considered too Indian a garment for Pakistanis) to perform the rousing poetic song by Faiz, '*Hum Dekhenge*' ('We shall see') in front of an electrified crowd of thousands in Lahore wearing a black *sari*. By then, the recently established (1981) Women's Action Forum had emerged at the forefront of articulating a response to Zia's oppressive regime; their aim was to strengthen women's rights, the restoration of democracy, and the promotion of a secular state (Figure 9). They were joined by other civil society organizations in voicing these demands, as well as for fuller rights of religious and minority groups. Expectedly, dissenting voices were punished, famously Fahmida Riaz (1946–2018), a leading

9. Protesters from the Women's Action Forum being baton charged by the police, Lahore, 1983.

feminist writer, poet, and activist, who was charged with sedition and forced into exile in India; only returning to Pakistan after Zia's death in August 1988.

The space for women and minorities shrank particularly during Zia's time in power, as he introduced the Hudood Ordinances, which repealed some of the British-era laws and replaced them with Sharia law. Infamously, these draconian measures made it incredibly difficult for women to prove rape, which often resulted in the victim being imprisoned instead of the perpetrator, because they were unable to provide the required four eyewitnesses of good standing to prove their innocence. The Ordnances also stipulated that a woman's testimony was only worth half that of a man (and in the case of non-Muslims, half and a quarter of that of a Muslim man for males and females respectively). Moreover, although rarely invoked, the new laws also included the punishment of stoning to death. Amid rising domestic dissent and international disgust, General Musharraf had these laws amended in 2006, when the Women's Protection Bill was introduced.

One of the criticisms of the Oxford-educated Benazir Bhutto, daughter of Zulfikar and the first female prime minister in the Muslim world, is that despite being the leader of the rhetorically progressive PPP, she failed to confront the religious fundamentalists in the country and made little effort to repeal the Hudood Ordinances. Her two terms in office (1988–90 and 1993–6) highlighted the strong underlying hand of the military apparatus, despite an outward semblance of democracy. And accusations of corrupt dynastic politics have abounded, as both her husband and son have remained key players in politics after her dramatic public assassination in 2007. Despite this, Bhutto still commands much affection and serves as a model of inspiration, inside and outside the country.

In more recent times, a few key women and events stand out. The human rights lawyer and social activist Asma Jahangir is often considered the conscience of Pakistan. She first emerged as a public figure when, in 1971, at the age of just 18, she took up the cause of her father's detention. Her father, Malik Ghulam Jilani, had been a vocal critic, especially of the military action in East Pakistan. She spent the rest of her life fighting for justice in Pakistan and built a career defending women's rights and minorities. A leading figure of the Women's Action Forum and the founding member of the Human Rights Commission of Pakistan, she used the legal profession to confront and challenge injustices in society, until her death in 2018.

More familiar to many in the West is Malala Yousafzai, who in 2009, as a school-going young teenager, wrote a blog for the BBC about the Pakistan Taliban's growing influence in her native Swat. She shared experiences of school closures for girls in the region, where the local Taliban leader, Maulana Fazlullah, had grown powerful through his vitriolic sermons on pirate radio against 'un-Islamic' practices. His followers targeted hundreds of schools, forcing girls to remain at home. Although Malala used a pseudonym, by the end of the year her identity was revealed, and she became openly critical of the Taliban. But it was the attempt on her life by the Taliban in 2012, which left her close to death, that catapulted her to international fame, made her the poster-girl in the West for advocacy work, and saw her receive the Nobel Peace Prize in 2014.

Malala is not without her critics in Pakistan. There is scepticism about her real contributions from afar, and some see her as taking refuge abroad for personal gain, while maligning the name of Pakistan. But this is a common trope. Most outspoken women in Pakistan, or writing critically about Pakistan, have been labelled as traitors, foreign agents, westernized, and out of touch with reality on the ground in the country. This accusation was even levelled against a gang-rape victim, Mukhtaran Mai, in 2002, who, instead of remaining silent, or committing the customary suicide, confronted her rapists and challenged the authorities to take action against a patriarchal and tribal system of 'honour revenge'. Her struggles brought her international attention and national unease, at the hands of an ambivalent judiciary and a suspicious military state.

The existence of a handful of such women, who spark the moral conscience of a society, may not make for sustainable and structural difference, but they capture wide attention, and on such examples hangs the hope for countless others engaged in the daily battle of challenging oppression and deeply ingrained inequalities, in which women are reduced to being the markers of national identity or tribal and family honour. Zia attempted to erase women out of school textbooks and keep them hidden from public spaces. The impact of his efforts remains but debates about gender have now been intersected by those between 'modernity' and 'tradition', West and East, Islamic and non-Islamic, and 'national' and 'foreign'. Since 2018, the Women's Action Forum and numerous other women's organizations have been actively marching in the streets across Pakistan to mark International Women's Day. This annual *Aurat* March has successfully rattled the exploitative patriarchal structures in Pakistan with provocative slogans such as *Mera Jism, Meri Marzi* ('my body, my choice'). At the same time, it has drawn criticism from religious right-wing parties and beyond, highlighting the challenges that still lie ahead.

Chapter 6
Visualizing the land of the pure

While the creation of Pakistan was a political project, hidden within it was another question that received less searching attention. What was (to be) Pakistan's 'national culture'? What was the cultural counterpoint to the political project? In September 1944, Jinnah swept around this, when writing to Gandhi that the Muslims were a nation and *not* a minority:

> We are a nation of a hundred million, and, what is more, we are a nation with our own distinctive culture and civilization, language and literature, art and architecture, names and nomenclature, sense of value and proportion, legal laws and moral codes, customs and calendar, history and tradition, aptitude and ambitions; in short, we have our own distinctive outlook on life and of life.

A year later, in the 1945–6 provincial polls a slogan emerged that represented this succinctly: *Pakistan ka matlab kya, La Ilaha Illallah* ('what does Pakistan mean? No God but Allah'; couplet from a poem by Asghar Sodai). This then was perhaps the common perception, if not the consensus, among the Muslim community in late colonial India vis-à-vis questions of political representation, if not yet of separation. The problem was that once separated from India, the two culturally diverse wings of Pakistan were geographically separated by India. Internally too, these wings had people who had uprooted (voluntarily or otherwise) and travelled there to create a new promised land. Amidst this diversity (of locals and migrants), it was religion and the concomitant desire to have a representative homeland for Indian Muslims that had brought them together and that was supposed to keep them united (as it turned out, not for long). Carving out a 'national culture' from these layers of ethnicities, linguistic identities, and regional affiliations, while simultaneously trying to clearly and cleanly distinguish oneself from the historical baggage associated with (pre-Partition) India, proved to be complicated and contradictory.

Literature, language, and politics

Questions around the search for crafting a national cultural identity, with a simultaneous need to (re)create history, arose soon after independence. Answers were attempted from a wide ideological spectrum, among whom were Wheeler and his patron, Fazlur Rahman from East Pakistan, who was the first minister for education (1947–53). A lawyer and an educationist from Dhaka and Calcutta universities and a member of the Royal Asiatic Society of Bengal, who became the president of the Pakistan Historical Society, Rahman insisted that a broader study of Islam should be at the heart of any programme. Within ten years, Jamil Jalibi, a scholar of Urdu from the United Provinces, wrote critically of this approach, terming it neo-colonial superseding the indigenous: 'Our independence interlaced with the partition of India has meant that we either look to Europe for modern culture or try to retrieve it from the archaeological remnants in Mohenjodaro, Taxila and Harappa, which were originally discovered by Mr Wheeler.'

If Pakistan were to claim this long history, it also meant embracing a diverse and intermingled history. On the other hand, if a more 'Islamic' culture was desired, then this long history was problematic. This debate echoed the two competing tendencies of Muslim nationalism, namely those of Sir Sayyid Ahmad Khan and Maulana Maududi, which still remain current. Sir Sayyid was the 19th-century intellectual who advocated western style education and established the Mohammedan Anglo-Oriental College, Aligarh, for this pursuit of rational science and internal reform, and influenced Jinnah and Iqbal. Maududi, a 20th-century thinker and founder of the JI, desired a return to a form of 'pure Islam' with Sharia law. With the break-up of Pakistan in 1971, Maududi's ideas got a stimulus, gained currency, and, to an extent, made answering the above questions simpler and clearer. Indeed, the view of two regions of Indus/Indic culture has been substantiated further after 1971, because western Pakistan is a far more natural (and feasible) entity than the two separate regionalized wings.

In 1968, Faiz Ahmed Faiz, Pakistan's poet laureate, produced a report, which would later become the blueprint for Pakistan's cultural policy under Bhutto. Although a left-wing intellectual who won the Lenin Peace Prize in 1962, and an atheist, it was impossible for Faiz to avoid the question of faith in framing policy. He stressed the importance of Islam but, crucially, did not end there. He continued that while they shared a common faith, the people of Pakistan also shared 'distinctive cultural traits of their own which distinguish them as a society and a nation from their co-religionists elsewhere'.

The Faiz Report led to the establishment of Pakistan's National Council of Arts in 1973. This new cultural policy emerged in an era that also saw the rise of the Pakistan Television Corporation (PTV), the sole state-run channel in the country from the mid-1960s for thirty years, in addition to a spread of cinema and radio, through all of which media popular culture also spread. These new platforms allowed Zulfikar Ali Bhutto to promote his brand of a Pakistani cultural identity, something that was both more important and less difficult, now the eastern wing was no longer part of the equation. Since this attempt at formulating a national cultural policy, there has been little investment in either planning or promoting the creative industries, which in part explains the decline in subsequent decades. The liberalization of the media in 2000 has been a significant landmark in terms of diversifying but also diluting the voices, content, and discussion. The decision to liberalize mass media was made by Musharraf and it is the military establishment that continues to watch over the watchdog; self-censorship amidst shrinking free speech is a common facet of present-day Pakistan. An equally important factor behind the decision to liberalize and open up the media was that Musharraf felt Pakistan had lost the information and cultural war to India and needed to create new platforms.

Whereas Faiz was mindful that any 'national culture' had to diffuse through dialogue rather than be imposed from the top, state education was an important institutional chain-of-command to produce, propagate, and instil the ideology of Pakistan. It was here that the subject 'History' was replaced by 'Pakistan Studies' in 1971, the latter made compulsory in the curriculum from schools through to university. It was both a symbolic shift and substantial change in that it focused on the entirety of Pakistan's existence, while leaving out inconvenient truths. While it acquainted the learner with the ancient Indus Valley Civilization, it leapt between the succeeding periods thereafter, to fast-forward to the Pakistan Movement. The curriculum assumed a more Islamic slant under Zia. This process of historical revisionism has been crucial in creating a monolithic and homogeneous Pakistan. The legacy of a selective writing and teaching of history is pervasive in the subcontinent and feeds the root of much of the religious nationalism, across borders. Still, no state project in a region of such diverse peoples, with their strong tradition of orality and visual cultures, can completely erase these multiple threads that form the cultural roots of Pakistan.

Between the reel and real

In 1913, the first silent movie, *Raja Harishchandra* ('King Harishchandra', dir. Dadasaheb Phalke), was produced in British India, and the first 'talkie' *Alam Ara* ('The Ornament of the World', dir. Ardeshir Irani) followed in 1931. By 1947, the film industry was well established in the cities of Bombay, Lahore, and Calcutta, producing films in the popular lingua franca of Hindustani, alongside Bengali and Punjabi. Lahore saw its first (silent) film, *The Daughter of Today*, in 1924 (dir. Shankradev Arya). Through this time, there were nine cinema houses in Lahore. The creation of Pakistan prompted or forced many artists and technicians in the film industry(s) to choose between the two countries. This travel of film culture in particular took place between Bombay and Lahore and, among others, saw the playwright Saadat Hasan Manto (1912–55), the prolific cataloguer of the pathos of Partition, the music composer Master Ghulam Haider (1908–53), and the singing superstar Noor Jehan (1926–2000) move to Pakistan. Lakshmi Chowk, in the heart of the walled city of Lahore, became the focal point for the industry, with cinemas, distributors, producers all located in the vicinity, with easy access for many of the stars who also lived in the area. The returning traffic saw Lahore-based producers like Roop K. Shorey and Dalsukh M. Pancholi leave the city. The latter's studio, Art Pictures, was left in the custody of his legal adviser, who went on to produce *Teri Yaad* ('Your Memories', dir. Daud Chand), Pakistan's first film, in 1948.

There persisted a somewhat surreal expectation for some time in the late 1940s and the early 1950s that the new political division would not disrupt the common heritage of art, craft, literature, music, and cinema. Indian films continued to be imported for a brief while albeit with customs duty. While this was good for the cinemagoer in Pakistan, it was not so good for the producers, and their agitation, in addition to worsening intergovernmental relations with India in 1950, saw an uncertain stop–start scenario, which was not helped by the state's attitude to the film industry. In 1949, the Pakistani minister of industry, Sardar Abdur Rab Nishtar, declared that 'in principle Muslims should not get involved in filmmaking. Being the work of lust and lure, it should be left to the infidels…'. The trouble was that even watching films depended upon the mercurial relationship with India. The government see-sawed between allowing Indian films into the Pakistani market and banning them or prohibiting artistic collaborations, a situation which continues today.

While the mid-1950s continued with a limited number of films produced and imported, with the onset of Ayub Khan's military regime, there was a spurt in home production. Amongst these, the most notable was *Jago Hua Savera* ('The Day Shall Dawn'), 1959. The film, directed by Lahore-based A. J. Kardar, was shot in Dhaka, East Pakistan, and its script, in Urdu, was by Faiz. A collaborative neo-realist film, it was acclaimed internationally but criticized at home for failing to capture the 'authenticity' of rural East Pakistan. *Jago Hua Savera* is memorable also for being the first Pakistani film to be submitted for nomination to the Academy Awards. With the exception of *Ghoonghat* ('The Veil', dir. Khurshid Anwar, 1962), there were no other submissions to the Oscars until 2013, when *Zinda Bhaag* ('Run Alive', dir. Farjad and Meenu) was submitted (Figure 10).

Although the period of Ayub Khan's government is considered to be 'modern' and 'progressive', the reality was that when the film *Jago Hua Savera* premiered in London, Faiz was prevented from attending. In 1954, the year in which the Communist Party of Pakistan was banned, *Roohi* ('Soulful', dir. W. Z. Ahmed) also became the first film to be banned by the Pakistan Film Censor Board. A largely imagined fear of socialism was the reason behind this decision. Ideological fears coupled with the reticent religious leadership ensured that the industry continued to meander through the 1960s. Looking back, the period appears somewhat of

Visualizing the land of the pure

10. Film poster for *Zinda Bhaag*.

a plateau if not a peak, given what followed thereafter—first under the populist Bhutto and then the theocratic Zia. This is poignantly captured in *Khamosh Pani* ('Silent Waters', dir. Sabiha Sumar, 2003), which revisits both the impact of Zia's Islamization and the shadows of 1947, still lurking around at the time.

Interestingly, the 1970s saw a rise of regional cinema, especially in Punjabi and Pashto languages. Indeed, this cinematic decade belonged to the legendary character of *Maula Jat* (dir. Yunus Malik, 1979), played by actor Sultan Rahi. He became a hugely popular character; rustic, an embodiment of the common man, dressed in the traditional *lungi-kurta*, and ready to fight all social evil. At the same time the film sparked the genre of hyper-violence in Punjabi films, but also perhaps signalled the dominance of the Punjabis following the break-up of Pakistan in 1971. Badar Munir, the Pashto equivalent of Sultan Rahi, had emerged on the silver screen in 1968. He starred in a 1973 film, *Urbal* ('Fire', dir. Mumtaz Ali Khan), which was hugely successful in KP and introduced and popularized the trend of violence and of gyrating dances by women in Pashto cinema. In the deeply conservative KP, this provided pseudo-erotic entertainment for men.

In his influential work on Pakistani cinema, Mushtaq Gazdar argues that characters such as Maula Jat, a downtrodden peasant, were symbolic of the repression provoked by martial law in 1977. The decade that had begun with the loss of the eastern wing was to end with the Soviet invasion of Afghanistan, bringing in a drug and gun culture. Alongside Iran's Revolution and its turn towards state religiosity, this was an impulse which started to permeate cultural spaces, even as they became patronized by the Zia regime. There was already complete censorship of the press, radio and TV were under state control, and the glamorization of violent heroic figures dealing with the problems in society resonated with people who were otherwise constrained.

With the break-up of Pakistan and political shifts taking place in the 1970s, the decline set in for the film industry. Apart from losing a valuable market, the number of films being produced declined from 114 in 1970 to 79 films released in 1971. While the Zia era promoted social piety and religiosity, the actual numbers of films released remained steady; 83 films released in 1977 compared to 84 in 1988 when he died. The impact, however, permeated society gradually and the more detrimental decline occurred in the late 1990s and interestingly concluded during the more 'secular' Musharraf period in the more turbulent era of post 9/11. By the end of Musharraf's period in power in 2008 only 36 films were released. Reflecting the broader decline of the film industry was the closure of cinema halls, which dropped from 493 in 1998 to a paltry 106 by 2007. Instead, they were giving way to a new substitute: former cinema halls were being transformed into shopping malls. Naz Cinema in Karachi was one of the first to be converted into Naz Plaza. Both independent and state-sponsored cinema, often infused with strong patriotism and propaganda, has undergone something of a revival since, but nothing comparable to its status before Zia, whose shadow is now arguably longer than that cast by Jinnah.

Combined with the social change taking place was the impact of technology. New technology in the form of the VCR player, which also brought piracy (especially of foreign films), growth of television, and more recently streaming, have effectively killed the film industry in Pakistan and confined film-watching to the private, cheaper, and safer spaces of home. However, it was the explosion of new cable TV channels following liberalization that dramatically changed the small screen. Particularly notable was the appearance of the risqué character of Begum Nawazish Ali, a high society lady, in programmes which aired between 2005 and 2007 on Aaj TV. The *Late Night Show with Begum Nawazish Ali* was hosted by Ali Saleem in drag, and greatly extended the boundaries of conversation (and criticism), raising issues of homosexuality and transgender through humour and innuendo. While Begum Nawazish was popular with Indian audiences too, it was the Pakistani dramas catapulted by the Zindagi channel in India that provided Pakistan programmes with a new platform and following from 2014. Pakistani serials and dramas are often considered more mature and sophisticated than their Indian counterparts, and significantly they helped to cut across the political divide and demystify the 'other'. This period of cultural collaboration and connection proved short-lived, as ties were severed following the attack on an Indian army brigade in Uri in September 2016. Pakistani stars such as Fawad Khan and Mahira Khan, who had successfully crossed over to mainstream Bollywood cinema, were dramatically dropped and banned in the hyper-nationalist milieu.

Blurring the line between the reel and the real have been the films and dramas made by Inter Services Public Relations (ISPR), the media wing of the Pakistan army. Established in 1949, ISPR has moved beyond just broadcasting and coordinating news on behalf of the military and also produces entertainment for mass consumption. This includes dramas such as *Alpha Bravo Charlie* (1998), annual Independence Day songs, and action-packed, patriotic films like the hugely successful *Waar* ('Strategy', dir. Balal Lashari, 2013), all designed to instil a sense of narrow nationalism. Collectively, these media productions by ISPR show the move towards a stronger, single ideological position in which simultaneously the space for individual creativity has shrunk. There are exceptions, such as *Khuda Kay Liye* ('For the Sake of God', dir. Shoaib Mansoor, 2007), which was one of the highest grossing films in recent times. Made in the post-9/11 climate, it explores the issue of extremism, presenting a nuanced and 'moderate Islam' for audiences at home and abroad. In January 2020, however, Sarmad Khoosat, one of the more successful directors in contemporary Pakistan, refused to release his film *Zindagi Tamasha* ('Circus of Life') to avoid a ban on the film. The film, 'about a struggling cleric shunned after a video of him dancing at a wedding goes viral', caused a furore following the release of its trailer, and Khoosat received many threats from Khadim Hussain Rizvi, an Islamic scholar and founder of the far-right political party Tehreek-e-Labbaik Pakistan, who asserted that the film 'might lead [people] to deviate from Islam and the Prophet' and accused Khoosat of blasphemy.

Naya Pakistan?

Equally paradoxical and perplexing is the relationship the Pakistani state has with music. The country has produced some of the most widely recognized and globally popular *qawwali* (Sufi devotional song) performers of modern times, such as Abida Parveen, Badar Ali Khan, Fareed Ayaz and Abu Muhammad, Nusrat Fateh Ali Khan, Rahat Fateh Ali Khan, and the Sabri Brothers, amongst many others. Pakistan has counted among its musical riches some of the greatest poets of the (semi) classical *Ghazal* form and, in contemporary times, has often been a leading theatre for pioneering, experimenting pop musicians, as compared to the vast and mostly vapid Bollywood popular music machine from India. Yet at the same time, theological debates continue about the extent to which music is either *haram* ('forbidden') or *halal* ('acceptable') in an Islamic country, thereby blighting not just social pleasure but also national treasures and international 'soft capital'.

The medieval tradition of Islamic mysticism has for centuries expressed itself in a lyrical form in an oral, vernacular society of myths and memories, legends and ballads, odes and epics. The *Raag*-based northern (Hindustani) form of classical music of the subcontinent, composed and improvised by traditional *gharanas* (loosely, schools or families of music), and patronized by the old courtly culture and the new colonial capitalists, has been the crowning jewel of Indo-Islamic syncretism. The highbrow three-part musical form of *khayal-dhrupad-thumri* vocals with instrumental accompaniment of *tabla-sitar-pakhawaj*, which emerged from roughly the 13th century, had a more popular and less restrained counterpart in Qawwali, performed more at shrines of Sufi mystics (pirs) than at the courts of princes.

Nusrat Fateh Ali Khan, born in 1948 in Faisalabad, Punjab, is widely regarded as the greatest and most global of *qawwals*, with a family pedigree and musical lineage that go back 600 years. Emerging in the 1970s with his troupe, he subsequently burst on the western international music scene with the help of a British music company, Oriental Star Agencies, which presented him to a wide audience beyond the subcontinental diaspora. In 1985, he performed at the WOMAD (World of Music, Arts, and Dance) festival in London and thereafter continued to collaborate with international artists until his untimely death in 1997 at the age of 49 (Figure 11). Few other south Asian artists have crossed musical, geographical, religious, and generational boundaries the way he did; equally therefore, for some, none was a greater transgressor.

Before him, though, Partition had drawn a line between musicians, as with filmmakers. Khan's own family originally came

11. **Nusrat Fateh Ali Khan performing at WOMAD, 1985.**

from Jalandhar (Punjab, India), while one of the greatest exponents of *Ghazal* (poetry of love) in Pakistan, Mehdi Hassan (1927–2012), was also born in Luna (Rajasthan, India) to a musical family. Hassan's family suffered financially following its migration and, like many others, he did odd jobs before his first performance on Radio Pakistan in 1952 brought him into the public limelight. He sang a ghazal by Faiz Ahmed Faiz, *'gulon mein rang'* ('colours in the flower'), which won the hearts of many and went on to establish him as the 'King of Ghazals' (*Shehanshah-e-Ghazal*). Some years younger than him is Ustad Ghulam Ali (b. 1940), from Sialkot (Pakistani Punjab) and a disciple of his namesake Bade Ghulam Ali Khan of Patiala (Indian Punjab), one of the great aforementioned *gharanas*. His electrifying radio/stage performances in the 1960s and 1970s led to his songs subsequently being sought by the Indian film industry, thus taking his music to mass audiences across the border.

Noor Jehan, the 'Queen of Melody' (*Malika-e-Tarannum*), was born in 1926 in Kasur (Punjab, Pakistan). Trained in classical singing under Ustad Bade Ghulam Ali Khan, she went on to become a leading singer-actress in the Bombay film industry in the mid-1940s. She, along with her director husband Shaukat Hussain Rizvi, moved to Karachi after Partition and emerged as the leading female vocalist. Mehdi Hassan, Khan, and Noor Jehan formed part of an outstanding pre-Partition generation of musicians of the Hindustani classical tradition. Other famous names include Roshan Ara Begum, Amanat Ali Khan, Farida Khanum, and Iqbal Bano. Their music can neither be contained by national boundaries nor quarantined by religious strictures. Radio Pakistan and PTV played an important early role in taking music to the homes of people, thereby ensuring crucial space for artists and their creativity to flourish.

It is said that music has no language. For a country that started to strain on linguistic nationalism, the eastern wing of Pakistan too had a thriving tradition, which intermingled with the west. Runa Laila, born in 1952 in Sylhet (present-day Bangladesh), became a leading playback singer for Pakistani films, before moving to Bangladesh in 1974. Nayyara Noor, born in 1950 in Guwahati, Assam (India), moved to Karachi later that decade and made a name for her singing from the mid-1970s onwards, especially her renderings of Faiz's compositions. Within the widening rift between state and society there is evidence of tolerant spaces: singers like A. Nayyar, the Benjamin Sisters, S. B. John, and Salim Raza, all Christian and all achieving considerable success. Tensions and conflicts have challenged, even severed, many of the cultural links across the Pakistan–India–Bangladesh boundaries, but no history of music and musicians can be anything but transnational.

Alamgir Haq, called the 'Elvis of the East', was also of Bengali descent but he remained in Pakistan, where he pioneered the pop music scene before the emergence of Nazia Hassan, the 'Queen of Pop' who took the subcontinent by storm in 1980. Her meteoric career was remarkable for its cross-border collaborative elements, her success in Bombay films, and her presence in the British album charts. By the mid-1980s, brought up and based as she was in London, she represented an urban, if not elite, anomaly at a time when the Pakistani grass roots were being transformed by Zia. Determined to visually Islamize Pakistani society and its presentations, his regime required female presenters on PTV to cover their heads. The contradictions in Zia's state project existed side by side; the gendered element has only been on the rise since then. Zia's Pakistan also saw the emergence of another pop/rock band from Rawalpindi in 1986. Vital Signs included two students from Peshawar University and went on to become one of the most commercially successful bands. They were the precursor to the immensely popular *Junoon*, with their youth anthem *Dil-dil Pakistan* ('heart/love Pakistan'), the trajectory of whose lead singer Junaid Jamshed is tellingly representative of Pakistan then and now.

Jamshed, who was from Karachi, underwent a spiritual rebirth and went from being a pop icon to an Islamic preacher. In 2004, under the influence of the Tablighi Jamaat (a transnational missionary movement in existence since 1926, and operating with varying degrees of success across Muslim communities), he renounced music and devoted his life to religion, becoming increasingly vocal in sharing his puritanical views on various subjects. His uncle was one of the founding members of Prime Minister Imran Khan's political party, Pakistan Tehreek-e-Insaaf (PTI), in 1996. Jamshed, in this avatar, provided the PTI with its own anthem of 'Naya Pakistan', in which the PTI promised a new Pakistan, free of corruption and bringing justice for all. Jamshed's conversion captures the shift from broad-minded patriotism to zealous Islamic nationalism, symbolized by the PTI under Imran Khan but spearheaded by the new middle class of Pakistan.

By the time of Jamshed's death in an air crash in 2016, Zia's Pakistan had turned full circle. It had started with the hanging of a political leader, Zulfikar Bhutto, in 1979 and, outlasting Bhutto's daughter, her opponents—Zia's protégé Nawaz Sharif—and Musharraf, it had ended with Imran Khan, the epitome of Zia's vision for Pakistan. While the music scene is now perhaps recognized mostly by Coke Studio (sponsored by the soft drinks maker and set up as a franchise in 2008), there is far more palatable packaging and far less grounded politics in its productions, in keeping with the conformities, consumptions, and comforting confines of the new middle class. Whatever organic roots it presents, they are more cosmetic and less creative. Ammara Maqsood terms this 'buying modern', a musical idiom in which Sufi sounds are strummed to an electric guitar and the new aspiring middle class can connect modernity with religiosity.

Outside the cities of Lahore and Karachi, dissent and disillusionment drive people to cling to subversive music as a medium. But the persisting traditions are too diverse, dispersed, and localized to enthuse and mobilize as did once the charisma, force, and passion of Nusrat Fateh Ali Khan or Iqbal Bano.

Piety and profanity

Located in the heart of the walled city of Lahore, overlooking the Badshahi Mosque, is Heera Mandi, the diamond market (Figure 12). During the Mughal period, Heera Mandi was seen as the cultural centre of the city, where the traditional 'courtesan' dance form known as *mujra* was performed by skilled courtesans, and considered an art. Through the colonial period, and afterwards, however, the line between the *mujra* and prostitution became blurred. In recent years, the area has been sanitized and given a facelift, and it now functions as a popular food street full of eateries, of which the most famous and established is Cuckoo's Den.

12. **Badshahi Masjid, Walled City of Lahore, constructed by Emperor Aurangzeb, 1673.**

Created by the artist Iqbal Hussain, Cuckoo's Den sits between the two extremes of piety and profanity, with all its contradictions laid bare. The building was once the home of courtesans, who charmed the local nobility and elites with their knowledge of poetry, dance, and classical music traditions, which was passed from one generation to the next. The courtesans, accompanied by *mirasis* (hereditary musicians), buckled under the pressures of the new religious state and the lack of patronage for their artistic form, and Heera Mandi increasingly turned to prostitution for survival. Hussain, himself the son, grandson, and brother of these 'dancing girls', painted these women and preserved the old mansion or *haveli*, while operating an eatery on the rooftops.

Heera Mandi, with its old havelis and narrow lanes set in the backdrop of grand 17th-century architecture, exudes the Mughal influences so prevalent in north India and Pakistan. The Mughal miniature style of painting was revived by Abdul Rahman Chughtai (1897–1975), Pakistan's first major artist. In keeping with the idea of Muslim self-determination, he rejected the modernist influences emerging from Europe and America. Ajaz Anwar, a Lahore-based painter, born in Ludhiana (India), has followed with work that pays homage to Lahore, trying desperately to preserve the old crumbling buildings on canvas. Anwar had spearheaded the Lahore Bachao (save Lahore) movement against the construction of the Orange Line Metro, which was finally inaugurated in October 2020. This bulldozing of history through the erasure of heritage sites in the name of new developmentalism is seen as disregard for Lahore's multicultural past and has been vehemently challenged by those who wish to preserve it. These voices are becoming fewer, and marginal to the wider desires of a burgeoning metropolis.

Under Zia, moral policing and cracking down on obscenity was part of the state project to control the personal and political lives of the people. Representation of what is deemed 'un-Islamic' or 'obscene', was quickly picked up by censors. Increasingly, music and dancing were presented as lewd, vulgar, and immoral acts which go against the tenets of Islam and should therefore be discouraged. This also marked a distinct rejection of these traditions, which have their roots in the subcontinental civilizations. During this period, when dancing in public was completely banned, many established artists sought exile and left Pakistan. When the kathak dancer Nahid Siddiqui's programme was pulled off air following the ban on dancing, she left for the UK, where she continued to perform. Sheema Kirmani, trained in the south Indian dance form of Bharatanatyam, continued regardless, and through the establishment of the Tehrik-e-Niswan ('The Women's Movement') used cultural activism and performance to raise social awareness. Others, who could not flee or chose to remain, confined themselves to private performances. The creative freedom and space for writers and artists was curtailed and they were forced to refrain from commenting on politics. Television and radio programme scripts were both vetted by an Islamic scholar and also sent to the Ministry of Information for approval. More airtime was devoted to religious programming, reinforcing the piety of the state.

The 1970s were a crucial decade in Pakistan, as it saw the transition from two wings to one and the shift from its first democratically elected prime minister to probably the most ideologically influential martial law regimes. The scars of this decade have been deep, divisive, and detrimental. If Ayub's Pakistan was a so-called 'golden age' of modernity and technology and Yahya's Pakistan was an age of 'blood and iron' especially in Bangladesh, then between Bhutto and Zia, the country saw its political, socio-cultural, and economic landscape transformed. From Bhutto hosting the second Islamic Summit conference in 1974 to the 'military-Islamic' dictatorship of Zia, which he himself fell prey to, this period saw the emergence of a new kind of Pakistan: culturally conservative and religiously literal, at least outwardly.

Small changes began to seep into mainstream society. The Persian parting greeting of *Khuda Hafiz*, roughly translated as 'may God protect you', was gradually replaced with the more Arabic sounding *Allah Hafiz*, which was first used on PTV in 1985 at the end of a programme. In contemporary social interaction, *Khuda Hafiz* is used by many to make a political statement against this encroachment from Arabia. The word *Khuda* represents more than just a simple greeting. It is a connection to the past, to the language and sentiments of poets like Iqbal and Faiz. It is part of the subcontinental Islamic tradition that developed over centuries rather than a recent injection. Similarly, the holy month of *Ramzan* has become *Ramadan*. The trend is so pervasive that Pakistan is sometimes referred to as 'Al-Bakistan' by critics and supporters alike (Arabic does not have the sound 'p', which is replaced with a 'b').

Away from the patron–client state and its glitz and glamour are the everyday spaces of the tea houses, street food, street art, and the underground, where subversive voices discuss the country's woes. Sometimes these subversive voices break out of the shadows, as with *The Sensational Life and Death of Qandeel Baloch* by the journalist Sanam Maher. Based on the extraordinary life of Baloch, a 26-year-old woman whose outspoken social media posts and provocative videos had outraged conservatives and who was murdered by her brother in 2016, the book highlights the stark contradictions in societal norms in Pakistan today. Baloch's life and death highlight the precarious relationship between popular culture, classist society, patriarchal family, and a strong religious state.

Chapter 7
The world outside

In May 1963, Zulfikar Ali Bhutto, then Minister for External Affairs of Pakistan, declared:

> Pakistan has arrived at peaceful settlement with all neighbouring countries, like China, Nepal, Afghanistan and Burma, except, unfortunately, India, which refuses to make the necessary adjustments to bring lasting peace to the subcontinent. I hope we can give undivided attention to one question which Pakistan faces—solution of the Kashmir problem.

This quote remains relevant, even today. The political idea of Pakistan, propagated from 1940 on, and which bore quick, if blighted, fruit in 1947, had roots in regions which, as we saw at the start of this narrative, had connections to the outside world through the seas and by land. The Arabian Sea, the Persian Gulf, and the Bay of Bengal, on the one hand, and the Silk Road, the Khyber Pass, and the Great Trunk Road on the other, had served as corridors for ideas, goods, and armies for thousands of years. Contemporary political imaginations, Cold War geopolitical relations, and post-Cold War globalization are variations on older themes. However, there has been one important change: while previously this ancient land was seen as one of opportunity to which people were drawn, today it is mostly the opposite.

Love thy neighbour?

Within two months and ten days of Partition, in October 1947, the governments of India and Pakistan were at an 'undeclared' war over one of its items of unfinished business: the then-princely state of Jammu and Kashmir. Pakistan feared that Jammu and Kashmir, among the largest, most strategically located of regions, would accede to India. Communal relations in the state were difficult: an unpopular Hindu Maharaja of the Dogra Dynasty ruled over a Muslim-majority population whose most popular leader nursed an ambition of regional self-determination. Theoretically free at the end of British paramountcy (1858–1947), the 550+ princely states in the subcontinent were effectively at the mercy of the rising tide of mass populism on the one hand, and the relevant imperatives of their geography, demography, military, and ideology, on the other.

The case of Jammu and Kashmir was especially sensitive. For Pakistan, it was difficult to imagine a border area with a Muslim-majority population belonging to India, given the two-nation theory and its logical conclusion in the Partition of British India. For India, by the same token, it was important to ideologically refute Pakistan's *raison d'être* by showing that India was a country for *all* communities. The Kashmiri ruler, veering between dreams of independence and declaration for India, saw sections of his population rise against him, soon aided and abetted by tribesmen entering from Pakistani territory. As he sought military assistance from India, New Delhi extracted the political price of accession to India and Karachi responded accordingly, triggering the first India–Pakistan war. Amidst this power play, the Kashmiri people living in the famed Vale of Srinagar but also in other regions like Jammu, Poonch, and Gilgit-Baltistan were caught up in this India–Pakistan binary.

Since then, stereotypes of Kashmir's scenic beauty, torn between the two rivals competing for the territory, have set the tropes of this dispute, be it in academia or fiction, such as Salman Rushdie's novel *Shalimar: The Clown*. This has thwarted an understanding of Kashmiri nationalism while not ushering in any kind of peace—with or without honour—in the region. Periods of surface calm have been underlain by passages of occupation and challenges to it. Meanwhile, on the map, the ceasefire line of 1949 turned into the Line of Control of 1972 and, on the ground, Kashmir remains trifurcated, with the Kashmiri people split between an India-administered, a Pakistan-held, and a China-controlled triangle. Neither of the principal parties has dared to hold a plebiscite in any part of the state. This denial of national self-determination to 12 million people militarized by India, and 4 million people by Pakistan, has seen demands of *Azadi* (freedom) on both sides, albeit more in India.

After successive waves of uprising from the late 1980s to the late 2010s, on 5 August 2019, the government of India, under the Hindu nationalist government of the Bharatiya Janata Party (BJP), revoked the state's special status and reduced it to directly controlled union territories. The government of Pakistan, meanwhile, has its own arrangements for the part of Kashmir under its administration, as well as the northern areas adjacent to Chinese Xinjiang called Gilgit-Baltistan. Greater integration of these Kashmir(s) with India and Pakistan is afoot, which papers over the fact that this is one of the most militarized regions in the world. India's grave human rights abuses in the valley of Kashmir for at least the past thirty years have been met with Pakistan's perennial Janus-faced approach to the issue: covert support and overt rhetoric for helping the angry young men perpetuate their conflict, but towards whose desired end?

The toxic mix of elevated nationalism and religion, but also petty political dishonesty, has meant that the Kashmir valley may well be on its way to becoming a bigger version of the Gaza Strip or the West Bank, if not Tibet. The administrative shifts taking place are clear, with the Indian state's desire for a form of settler-colonialism paralleling the demographic change achieved in Tibet by the Chinese state since 1959, and by the Israeli state in Palestine. Four wars (1947, 1965, 1971, 1999), almost daily border skirmishes, tit-for-tat meddling in insurgencies (Kashmir, Balochistan, Indian Punjab), and the hyper-masculine nationalism sweeping across the subcontinent see majoritarian loyalty to these authoritarian states (Figures 13 and 14).

If the end of empire was far from clean, then the emergence of the Cold War in the region was equally messy. Pakistan courted the USA before and under Ayub Khan in the 1950s–1960s, while Zulfikar Bhutto increasingly looked towards Mao's China and the Organization of Islamic Conference in the 1970s. Zia received a God-sent opportunity in the Soviet invasion of Afghanistan, which renewed US interest in Pakistan after 1979, while the Saudi Royal House, long close to the USA, was also keen to nip in the bud any

13. Official border crossing at Attari (India) and Wagah (Pakistan). The checkpost has been expanded since 2006, when this picture was taken.

14. Pakistani Rangers from the flag-lowering ceremony at Ganda Singh Wala border, Kasur, 2017.

varieties of 'socialism', no matter if Islamic. Zia's vision for Pakistan was the perfect fit for the Saudis and what emerged was an alliance of religious parties, strategic interests, and despotic leaderships—all bankrolled by American and petro-dollars. All this was simultaneously strained and strengthened by the rise of the Taliban and al-Qaeda in the 1990s–2000s.

Since 2000, Pakistan has been hyphenated increasingly less with India and more with its other neighbour, Afghanistan. They share a 1,500-mile border that in parts is soft and porous, with overlapping ethnicities and socio-cultural practices. Much more than the mid-20th-century Radcliffe Line with India, Pakistan's political relationship with Afghanistan has been bedevilled by the late 19th-century Durand Line—a colonial artefact that has been contested by successive Afghan governments. They refused to accept the loss of territories east of the Line and the consequent severing of the people's ties across this political boundary, and in 1947 Afghanistan was the only country to vote against the entry of Pakistan to the UN.

The idea of a greater Pakhtoonistan lived on for a while, carrying the legacy of the 'troubled frontier'—a colonial inheritance. Significantly, Pakistan has also been a refuge, hosting one of the largest refugee populations in the world. Afghans first started to flee en masse when Soviet forces stormed the Tajbeg Palace (Kabul) and assassinated the Afghan president Hafizullah Amin in December 1979. Eleven years later, there were an estimated 3.7 million Afghans in Pakistan. The civil war that followed the withdrawal of the Soviet troops and saw the Taliban take over government in Kabul by 1996 only enlarged this population, with accompanying challenges to house, feed, and employ them. Pakistan, along with Saudi Arabia, and the United Arab Emirates (UAE), was one of the first countries to recognize Taliban rule, and security studies literature abounds with descriptions of the Pakistani state's 'run with the hare and hunt with the hounds' role in its rise.

Any repatriation of refugees was halted by the events of 9/11 and the 'war on terror' from 2003. By then, the UNHCR estimated that 5 million Afghan refugees were in refugee camps in Pakistan. Of late, Pakistan's relationship with Afghanistan has waxed and waned, affected by American intentions, Indian interventions, and the investments of both. Perhaps the greatest legacy of this was Zia's survival in power until 1988, given the Americans' need for him to create a Vietnam for the Red Army in Afghanistan. Fifteen years later, US troops would be back in Afghanistan and this time among the beneficiaries would be another Pakistan general-turned-president, Pervez Musharraf.

In this repeating cycle of history, the ultimate price was paid by the people and places in Pakistan. The country was flooded by nefarious funds, weapons, and narcotics, often travelling between the seaport of Karachi and the gateway to the north, Peshawar. These cities have remained a hub for political, ethnic, religious, and drug-related violence, in which arms travelling to and from Afghanistan found a happy home. Apart from creating a culture of normalized everyday violence, the resulting volatility has weakened the economic position of Pakistan by inevitably deterring foreign investment.

While courting the West, chiefly Americans but also the British, from within or without the confines of the Commonwealth (Pakistan remains one of the biggest recipients of UK aid), Pakistan has also had a close relationship with Communist China. This so-called 'all weather friendship' was formally forged in 1963, when the two countries signed a border agreement delimiting the territory along the Karakoram Mountain Range. China has ever since proved to be a reliable friend in need, especially when the USA and the UK have not. After all, their alliance has as much, if not more, to do with countering India than with anything else. It was no coincidence that the 1963 agreement came soon after India was defeated in its 1962 war with China. Slightly prior to this, a partnership had started in 1959 to build the Karakoram Highway linking Kashgar, in Xinjiang, to Islamabad via the Khunjerab Pass, which follows the path of the ancient Silk Road.

The rather scenic highway was fully completed in 1978 and opened to the public in its entirety in 1986. The present Chinese government's Belt and Road Initiative builds, in many respects, on this example, with a larger-scale resurrection of the Silk Road through this region. At the south Asian heart of BRI is the China–Pakistan Economic Corridor (CPEC), which envisages Chinese investments in Pakistan amounting to $62 billion. Through this project, China will help in a wide spectrum of infrastructure projects, from power (electricity) to road and rail transport. The centrepiece is the development of the deep-sea Gwadar Port, on the far south-western coast of Balochistan. The administrative control of the port is handled by Pakistan's Maritime Secretary, while the operational control is held by the little-known China Overseas Port Holding Company. This provides China with an access to the Arabian Sea, Persian Gulf, and the Indian Ocean. In the making since 1998, work started in 2002 and was completed four years later. In many ways, it was the launch pad for the CPEC, which took off over 2013–15.

These substantial investments in Pakistan are crucial because Pakistan's economy has suffered significantly since 2001 and foreign investment in the country has dropped dramatically due to security concerns. After the election of President Trump, US assistance and aid programmes declined substantially. This drop has been countered by investments from the Saudi Crown, which has pledged $20 billion, and the UAE, pledging $3 billion. While Beijing has continued to be the 'all weather friend', the political price to be paid is also obvious. Most visible is the silence of Islamabad on the question of the treatment of the (Muslim) Uighurs in Xinjiang, China. Pakistan's refusal to criticize Beijing on their persecution is in contrast to its sharp criticism of human rights abuses in Kashmir, Palestine, and Myanmar.

The Pakistani diaspora

The overseas Pakistani community number around 9 million people, and half of those are based in the Gulf states. The UK has the largest Pakistani diaspora community outside the Gulf, with over a million people, while substantial numbers also live in the United States (500,000+) and Canada (200,000+). These groups have emerged from different waves of migration and settlement, often reflecting and responding to colonialism, the world wars, and regional changes. Given that this is one of the largest diaspora populations in the world, it has curiously drawn little academic research. This may be partly because the earlier phases of migration, until the 1970s, were often understood collectively within a South Asian context, while the post-1970s numbers have increasingly been incorporated within a global Muslim diaspora. But Pakistanis overseas are as diverse as their country and make a big contribution to the Pakistani economy via their remittances.

The Pakistani diaspora has developed largely since the 1970s, but smaller numbers also migrated following independence in 1947. Post-war reconstruction and labour shortages in the UK were an important factor in attracting men from the Commonwealth, including small numbers of Pakistanis. Equally important were professionals such as doctors. However, the majority of the Pakistani diaspora in the UK comes from Mirpur, a small district in its part of Kashmir. There has been a history of migration from this area since the 1940s, but following the construction of the Mangla Dam in the early 1960s there was a sharp increase. This was partly due to the displacement caused by the construction of the dam, but also because the British contractor behind the dam was assisting the displaced residents.

This cheap labour started life in manufacturing and shifted into the service sector, or, as Virinder Kalra put it in his influential work, *From Textile Mills to Taxi Ranks*, in northern British towns and in the 1970s–1980s sent back remittances that enabled Mirpur to prosper much more than the rest of Pakistan. Brand new markets catered for diaspora tastebuds, grand houses were built to display the newly acquired televisions and videos—all this in a small, remote area adjacent to north Punjab in rural Pakistan. With Mirpur being in the politically contested territory of Kashmir, there are layers to identity politics here. Mirpuris often identify themselves ethnically as Kashmiris, amidst whom is a strand that would like to see a nation of Kashmir independent of India *and* Pakistan. Their migration story is thus connected to wider questions of competing diasporic identity and Kashmiri nationalism.

Away from Britain, the Gulf has been the choice destination for the vast majority of Pakistanis. The oil boom of the 1970s propelled the old seafaring trade links across the Arabian Sea and through the Persian Gulf. People from large swathes across the subcontinent responded to the demand for labour in Saudi Arabia and the UAE. Many Pakistanis were eager to leave the grim economic conditions and mass nationalization of industry by Bhutto and were lured by the construction and developments taking place in the Gulf. The 'new middle class' in Pakistan can be considered in part a creation of this group and its financial injections into a fragile economy, enabling urban centres and rural development. This class is characterized by their disposable income and conspicuous consumption, reflected in the growth of restaurants, malls, multiplexes, etc. in urban cities and also a concomitant religious revivalism and spiritual piety. In 2019, the value of their remittances was $21.8 billion, with $5 billion from Saudi Arabia alone. Imran Khan's government, capitalizing on the PTI's popularity in the diaspora, has been encouraging Pakistanis overseas to remit back home to save the cash-strapped economy and to build *Naya* Pakistan.

The relationship between Pakistan and Saudi Arabia has only gone from strength to strength. In intergovernmental matters, the kingdom has offered Pakistan generous economic assistance, and in recent years, the two countries have been cooperating militarily too. The best illustration of this is the appointment in 2017 of General Raheel Sharif, Pakistan's former Chief of Army Staff (2013–16), as the commander-in-chief of the Islamic Military Counter Terrorism Coalition of thirty-nine countries, with its headquarters in Riyadh. As already noted, Saudi Arabia has had great impact on the religious and cultural landscape of Pakistan. Added to its substantial funding of *madrassas* (religious schools) that are closely aligned to a more puritanical version of Islam (*Ahl-e-Hadith*) practised there, is the symbolism of the iconic Shah Faisal Mosque, the largest in Pakistan, funded with $120 million from the kingdom in 1976 and named after King Faisal (Figure 15). Indeed, the design of the mosque by the Turkish architect Vedat Dalokay pays homage to the Arabian Bedouin tent. Then, there is the renaming of colonial Lyallpur as Faisalabad in 1979, after King Faisal. Faisalabad is not only one of the leading commercial centres in Pakistan, but also functions as a hub for entrepreneurs and overseas workers.

15. **Shah Faisal Mosque, Islamabad (built 1986).**

This relationship with Saudi Arabia, complementing the changes in Pakistan after the independence of Bangladesh, saw the Islamic dhow sail away from its subcontinental mooring. However, this assertion of a stronger Islamic identity of the Saudi brand has meant tetchy relations with the neighbouring Shi'a-majority Iran, as well as the more Europeanized Turkey. Whether it was the Iran–Pakistan natural gas pipeline (continuing into India) or the popularity of Turkish television dramas in Pakistani drawing rooms, amending the text of the penal code along Sunni Sharia lines is one thing; ignoring a near-neighbour and a more distant but long-standing influence (Turkish lore in subcontinental politics goes back to the Khilafat movement of a century ago) is quite another. Furthermore, relations with the kingdom have not always been smooth. Over half a million Pakistanis have been deported from Saudi Arabia between 2012 and 2019 over expired visas and other offences. In September 2019, Riyadh abruptly decided to reject postgraduate medical degrees from Pakistan. And in any case, working conditions in the Arabian Peninsula have never been appealing (there are numerous accounts of employers withholding passports, of unpaid wages, and poor working conditions). Despite all this, approximately 2.5 million Pakistanis live in Saudi Arabia. The allure of making it abroad to escape the immediate economic hardships at home is too strong.

The price that such escape can entail was brought home in the 2013 film *Zinda Bhaag* ('Run Alive', dir. Farjad Nabi and Meenu Gaur), which portrayed the issue of illegal migration painfully through the experiences of three friends, each of whom tried to cross borders illegally with the risk of death if they did not succeed. The film, representing the re-emergence of independent cinema, was Pakistan's official entry for the Best Foreign Language Film at the Academy Awards that year. The changing contours of the cinematic portrayal of Pakistan poignantly capture changing perceptions and identities, those of self and 'the other'. The comedy drama *East is East* (dir. Damien O'Donnell, 1999), set in Salford, UK, in 1971, brings to life the story of one family, headed by a Pakistani man, and the challenges of his children growing up in Britain. By contrast, the 2012 film *The Reluctant Fundamentalist* (dir. Mira Nair), based on Mohsin Hamid's novel, is a political thriller depicting the conflict between the American dream and a re-evaluation of self and its sovereignty in an American society that treats any Muslim with suspicion. The 'inside–outside' dichotomy of contemporary Pakistan is that of an increasingly Islamic country in an increasingly Islamophobic world.

Ziauddin Sardar, the British-Pakistani scholar, suggests that Pakistanis have a love/hate relationship with America. There are those who want to migrate there and, at the same time, the USA is also perceived as a meddling villain, especially since the 'war on terror' began. Of course, Pakistan has also received significant sums in American aid over the decades. Although the character Changez in Hamid's novel goes back to Pakistan, the real population of Pakistanis in the USA has only continued to grow. From 30,000 in 1980, it is now over half a million. Pakistanis in the USA mostly come from cities such as Lahore, Karachi, Rawalpindi, Faisalabad, Hyderabad, and Peshawar. Most have settled in New York, New Jersey, and California, seeking better opportunities, across 'white-collar' sectors. This group is different from those who have migrated to the UK and the Gulf states in terms of its class and cultural capital. But among this group are also the persecuted Ahmadiyyas, declared non-Muslim in 1974, as well as illegal migrants such as those depicted in *Zinda Bhaag*, who take on poorly paid jobs, becoming taxi drivers, newspaper vendors, waiters, and petrol pump attendants, all having been lured by the American dream.

In between the tectonic political shifts inside (Bangladesh, 1971) and outside (9/11), lay the Salman Rushdie affair of 1988–9. Rushdie, whose magical-realist novels related to Indian independence (*Midnight's Children*, 1981) and the creation of Pakistan (*Shame*, 1983), had touched these countries' sensitivities by taking on the life of the Prophet Muhammad in his fourth novel, *The Satanic Verses* (1988). With a *fatwa* calling for his death issued by the supreme leader of Iran in February 1989, the novelist became the news himself, overtaking the contents of his book, which had been banned in both India and Pakistan. As Ziauddin Sardar remarked, looking back on the episode twenty years later:

> The Rushdie affair had no place for reasoned Muslim opinion. It was structured on the assumption that those who question or criticise Rushdie's right to say what he said are by definition barbarians. Thus, the only valid Muslim opinion was the extremist one; and the only Muslim voices that could be heard were of those who supported the fatwa. This dynamic justified the perception that Islam represented, in Rushdie's words, 'the darkness of religion'.

This has presented a peculiar dilemma in Pakistan ever since, on themes such as internal reform, secularism, perpetual doubt, and, above all, as Ziauddin Sardar asked, whether 'a single way of being

Muslim can be a ray of light for all Muslims'. These questions have no easy answers and thus an escape—whether via pull or push factors—to wherever there is a potential for a better life abroad is an obvious attraction. More than the economic migrants, it is the individuals who are hounded or forced to flee for fear of persecution whose plight is disturbing.

Among these have been journalists speaking against the state—Pakistan is 145 out of 180 in the World Press Freedom Index (2020)—and members of the dwindling minorities, most recently the Christian woman Asia Bibi, who was acquitted on blasphemy charges but sought asylum in France in 2020. Others on the peripheries of the homogeneous society that is being forged include LGBTQ people. Although Pakistan's parliament passed a law in 2019 guaranteeing basic rights for transgender citizens, the social stigma attached to them in a discriminatory society leads to attacks, forcing many to seek sanctuary in the outside world.

Sport, politics, and social change

If there is one thing which sounds the jingoistic trumpets in India and Pakistan, it is cricket. The most popular sport in South Asia, cricket provides entertainment, money, hero worship (and villainy), and manages to rouse the mildest of nationalists. Equally, to many, this spectacle is a vulgar travesty; a distraction from the structural poverty and inequality in the region; verily an opium of the masses. It has usurped the place of field hockey—the 'official national game' that formed the source of bragging rights between the 1950s and 1970s, especially at the Melbourne (1956), Rome (1960), and Tokyo (1964) Olympic games, when India and Pakistan contested three successive finals. Pakistan's last gold medal was won at Los Angeles (1984) with the charismatic Hassan Sardar and the last medal (bronze) at Barcelona (1992) under centre forward Shahbaz Ahmed. In the same time-span, Pakistan also had two world champions in Jahangir and Jansher Khan in the game of squash.

16. Under Imran Khan's captaincy Pakistan won the Cricket World Cup in 1992.

Cricket (its popular one-day form in addition to the classical five-day version) emerged as the leading sport from the late 1970s and Pakistan, having co-hosted (with India) the World Cup in 1987, won the 1992 edition, under the captaincy of Imran Khan (Figure 16). The colonial roots of cricket in South Asia cannot be overlooked but the subcontinent (including Bangladesh and Sri Lanka) has made the game its own. Like the colonial rulers and their princely collaborators, cricket in British India remained a remote, urban, and elite preserve up until the 1930s, when India gained 'test' status and a team toured England.

In the aftermath of the Second World War, cricket resumed in late-colonial India, soon to be overtaken by the Partition disturbances. Afterwards, cricket ties were among the first to be resumed, and a Pakistan team travelled to India in 1952, for its maiden 'test' tour. In the next decade, the countries took turns to host each other but a majority of these games were 'drawn', as neither side could either overpower the other or, crucially, take risks to win, fearing a loss (of face). This was still better than what followed between 1961 and 1978, when there was a complete stoppage of play between the two countries, as political relations deteriorated.

Meanwhile, cricket's popularity continued in both countries, with PTV broadcasting matches from the late 1960s, paving the way for the more frenzied popular fan following that we associate with the game today. By 1978, the political climate had changed in both countries and, over the next five years, they regularly played each other. Ironically, it was the puritanical General Zia who most effectively used the idea of cricket diplomacy, with his message of 'cricket for peace', and journeying to Jaipur, India, in 1987 to watch a cricket match with the Indian Prime Minister Rajiv Gandhi, at a tense time of military standoff.

Through the late 1980s and the 1990s, as bilateral tours endured another barren decade, Sharjah, UAE, emerged as the 'home away from home' for the two teams, given its increasing expatriate population from the subcontinent. In between, in 1996, Pakistan again co-hosted (with India and Sri Lanka) a cricket World Cup and played its part in shifting the popular balance of power away from the traditional holders, the British (White) Commonwealth. The 1999 Pakistan trip to India came at a sensitive time, after the two countries had conducted their nuclear tests in 1998 and just before the Kargil war of summer 1999.

Acting as an icebreaker, the game at least provided a forum for some people-to-people exchange (sporting visas were issued). The years 2004–8, when Pakistan and India played four back-to-back bilateral tours, now appear a golden age. Since the terrorist attack in Mumbai in November 2008, the two countries have only played each other on foreign soil. What has been most striking is how much of this rivalry has seeped through into the general body politic and how much the administration of the game oozes with state propaganda. Therefore, the rather lucrative Indian Premier

League of the shortest, the most popular, and heavily monetized version of the game has excluded Pakistani players since its inaugural season in early 2008. Indeed, since the attack on the Sri Lankan team in Lahore in March 2009, Pakistan went an entire decade without hosting the international cricket community.

However, changes in attitudes are not limited to just this bilateral rivalry. The Pakistan team has also visibly changed, reflecting the wider transformation of society and the cultural landscape. The Pakistani journalist Nadeem Farooq Paracha has argued that cricket culture reflects the wider socio-political mindset. Cricket has been more than a mere game for the colonized countries in the subcontinent, as in the Caribbean. Pakistan's first cricket captain was the Oxford-educated Abdul Hafeez Kardar. Initially, the players were mainly from the two leading cosmopolitan centres, Lahore and Karachi. There was no representation in the national team from East Pakistan, despite having the majority population. In the past thirty years, the players' pool has widened to smaller towns and provincial areas.

One visible change over the years has been the players' public display of religiosity, most prominently exhibited and associated with the captaincy of Inzamam-ul-Haq (2003–7). From being the preserve of Oxford Blues and the Lahori landed elite, mingled with 'streetfighters' from Karachi, half the cricket team were now connected with the revivalist, millenarian Tablighi Jamaat movement. In 2008, it prompted a Pakistan journalist to write about 'the Islamisation of Pakistani cricket'. The Tablighi Jamaat's largely apolitical and humanitarian stance has proved to be particularly popular amongst the rising middle class in Pakistan. At the same time, its members wear their religiosity and mark their bodies and conduct, accordingly. In 2006, the Pakistan Cricket Board was forced to issue a warning to the players about striking a 'balance between religion and cricket'.

By contrast, state endorsement and social excitement has been muted when it comes to women playing sports. Although numbers are small and their public profile limited, nevertheless many women have been able to break the barriers despite the odds. In 1996, two young sisters, Shazia and Sharmeen Khan from Karachi, led the way in establishing a women's cricket team recognized by the Pakistan Cricket Board. Despite the backlash, which included death threats and court cases, the sisters cleared the path for the team's participation in the Women's World Cup in 1997. That women's cricket in Pakistan is much more accepted and has grown tremendously since was seen in the accolades that poured in on the retirement of former captain Sana Mir in 2020, after a fifteen-year international career as a premier all-rounder. But right-wing religious groups continue to target events such as the mixed marathon race in Gujranwala in 2005, which gained much attention in Pakistan and abroad. Sporting bodies have since sought to accommodate the concerns of religious conservatives by following strict dress codes, having segregated training facilities, and ensuring the safety of the players so that they can continue to participate in sports.

Today, nowhere is the motif of cricket in Pakistan more useful as a prism of social change than right at the very top: in the life and times of the present prime minister, Imran Khan. Born in 1952, Khan has roots from his maternal side that are now on the other side of the Radcliffe Line, in Jalandhar, India. He was born into a Pashtun family from Lahore, which already had cricket stars in his cousins, for example Majid Khan. After schooling in England and an Oxford degree, Khan made his debut in test cricket with the Pakistan team against England in June 1971, when Pakistan still had two wings, and would cap a glittering twenty-one-year career by winning the 1992 cricket World Cup. After raising money to establish the first cancer hospital in Pakistan in 1994, later his springboard into politics, he married into the Goldsmith family and established his political party, the PTI, in 1996.

What followed was a slow and to many a shocking twenty-two-year transformation from cricketing icon and playboy to pious philanthropist and conservative politician, who finally reached the top—with some help along the way from the military establishment—in August 2018. The colonial legacies were very much in evidence in 1971, when Imran Khan took his first steps in international cricket, representing a country barely twenty-five years old. It is apt in many ways that another rebirth of Pakistan is now taking place on his watch, even if not entirely at his behest. Imran Khan, with his spiritual mentor-spouse in *purdah* and his ever-visible rosary beads, represents this *Naya* Pakistan, which is youthful and restless, aspirational but also directionless, seeking to break through old barriers of land, class, and caste but also stymied by the military–industrial–religious complex. His successful conversion from a global icon to representing a narrowly defined nationalist Pakistan says more about the society in which he is embedded.

Chapter 8
Looking backwards, going forward?

When Imran Khan took office as prime minister of Pakistan in August 2018, he began his maiden address to the nation thus:

> There are two types of politics: one in which one would pursue his career, and the second, my role model, Quaid-e-Azam, Muhammad Ali Jinnah, who conducted politics for a mission, that our prophet Hazrat Muhammad brought revolution in the world's history by creating state of Madinah...an Islamic welfare state envisioned by Allama Muhammad Iqbal which have showcased in the comity of nations that what is real Islam.

After invoking these three historical figures and tying them by the thread of Islam, he went on to sketch plans for his *Naya* Pakistan. In its seventieth year, it seemed that the Islamic Republic of Pakistan had settled down to some kind of democratic pattern or, as some political scientists have suggested, a 'hybrid regime'. After seeing four spells of military rule in six decades, Pakistan had seen three successive elections since 2008. In these, a tripartite contest had been waged between the Pakistan People's Party of the Bhuttos, the Sharif brothers' Pakistan Muslim League (Nawaz), and Imran Khan's Pakistan Tehreek-e-Insaaf, with each winning in turn. This sustained democratic spell has, though, been under the twin shadows of the military and the mullah (religious leader). Bedevilled by political violence, blighted by severe political corruption, and beset by a tight-knit *biradari* (brotherhood/kinship) public sphere, the people have drawn unity from, in the words of historian Faisal Devji, the idea of 'belonging' to a land rather than belonging to it in its present form. Much as the old Pakistan Movement of the 1940s was in pursuit of a 'New Medina', so the new Pakistan of Imran Khan in 2020 seeks a 'Riyasat-e-Madinah' (state of Medina).

Jinnah's dream was powerful enough to become a reality, but it was also vague enough to be malleable in a disenchanting manner. As we have seen, weak institutions, lack of leadership, and, above all, conflicting ideas about how to build the 'land of the pure' opened up space for rigid structures and harsh ideologies to thrive. Beneath and beyond them, over generations, the restless young oscillated between agitation for their hopes and accommodation, with the attendant danger of disillusionment, born out of fear, insecurities, and inequities. Straddling these social fault-lines, and personifying some, Imran Khan came into office in 2018 on the promise of eradicating big-ticket corruption, overhauling Pakistan's seriously debt-ridden financial problems, and breaking away from 'the life-style of those in power'. He sought help from the youth, the Pakistani diaspora, and countries willing and able to help Pakistan, chiefly China and Saudi Arabia.

What is new about *Naya* Pakistan? Is it simply old Pakistan that has been dressed up in a new outfit? Or has anything fundamental changed? While ultimately only time can tell, anthropologist Ammara Maqsood and historian Ali Usman Qasmi have noted one key societal change, alongside structural continuity, in Pakistan's 'new middle class', which seems to have broken away from its predecessor in three significant ways. First, it has become politically more active than previously, when it was a passive observer and supporter of the military. Second, it has expanded considerably since the days of Zia, consolidating through the years of the Bhutto and Sharif premierships, and gathering strength during nearly a decade of Musharraf's government; state 'market-oriented' economics remained the same through all three phases. Third, as its voice became further magnified in the emerging echo chambers of social media, its socio-cultural ascendancy has been accompanied by a religious turn, one which, when yoked to nationalism, allowed the new middle class to shift away from the provincial client–patron networks of the older, feudal parties and helped propel Imran Khan to prime ministerial office, if not to power.

Among this ambitious class, and those aspiring to join their ranks, it is the youth, in particular, to whom Imran Khan owed his electoral victory in 2018. His old-new popularity amongst them, combined with their frustration with the clannish political parties of the Sharifs and Bhuttos, allowed him to embark on his long *Azadi* (freedom) March, following claims of election-rigging during the 2013 general election. According to a UN Development Programme (UNDP) report of 2018, 64 per cent of the country's population is below the age of 30. His political rhetoric and ability to capture a sense of the historic resonated among millennials and post-millennials, many of whom were voting for the first time in 2018, resulting in a vote for change. Like populist leaders before him, and those elsewhere, he pinned his hopes for the nation and political fortune on the potential of the youth, and the aspirational middle classes. For this support to materialize, however, poverty alleviation and social uplift policies are crucial. One-third of Pakistan's population still lives under the poverty line and it is ranked at 150/189 in the latest UN Human Development Index. Yet, its defence expenditure, one of the highest in the world, comfortably outweighs its commitment to education, which is one of the lowest.

Indeed, on all major socio-economic indicators—from mortality to literacy rates, from access to clean water, sanitation facilities, healthcare to electricity supply—country-wide figures are less than flattering. And they are further skewed among the regions by the rural/urban divide and by the gender divide. Overall, according to UNDP, 'multi-dimensional' poverty plagues Pakistani provinces—some more than others, such as FATA and Balochistan, but in all, between one-fourth and one-third of the population remains poor, and the situation is getting worse. This widening gap, keeping in mind that the young among the poor have only seen a post-Zia Pakistan, with its prominent military, all-permeating religion and pervasive intra-national/international conflicts, is the toughest of the intersectional challenges in Pakistan.

All this makes for a resilient society but also a restless one, seeking change. Regulating and monitoring dissent is a colonial inheritance in the region, and sedition laws of a different era have been carefully crafted to suit the purposes of the past seventy years. They are designed not just to detain protesters but also to deter those who question authority. Thirty-five years of military dictatorships and stop–start democratic infrastructure has at least led to a small, critical civil society. This group—generationally renewed by students and other young people—periodically bursts into life, as in that famous year of protest of 1968, when its uprising brought down the dictatorship of Ayub Khan in March 1969. Fifteen years later, in 1984, Zia banned student unions, no doubt fearing that history might repeat itself. As recently as 2018, a Student Solidarity March reawakened old state suspicions and resulted in some of the organizers being arrested. The group is an umbrella organization that demands a reinstatement of student union elections, an increase in education investment, and a lifting of the ban on students participating in political activities.

Protest in Pakistan is however not owned by critical youth. Organizations like the JUI (F) (split branch of Jamiat Ulema-e-Islam, 'Assembly of Islamic Clerics'), led by Fazal-ur-Rehman, a cleric-politician, who turned Imran Khan's brand of street-march protest-politics against him in 2019, and TTP (Tehreek-e-Taliban, the Pakistan Taliban), an armed group that has engaged the

Pakistani army along the Afghan frontier, continue to challenge the state. With the *muhajir* fault-line in Sindh, the nationalist fringe in Balochistan, and students across campuses in the country, various aspirational voices demanding change from their perspectives and through various methods are agitating quietly and publicly, making effective use of social media. In Pakistan, this is dominated by Facebook, which has an overwhelming market share of 94 per cent (2020), compared to Twitter's paltry—but no doubt rising—figure of 4 per cent. On the whole though, active social media users number around a fifth of a population of 220 million—a figure that is only going to rise, with smart phones enabling wider data connectivity. The use of new technologies presents challenges and opportunities, but it also exposes the gaps within society in terms of accessibility. Still, the trend here too is one way. In 2019, China Mobile Pakistan (CMPak Ltd), with its brand name Zong 4G, conducted Pakistan's first 5G tests, the first to do so in South Asia.

Apart from the enhanced censorious attempt by the state to keep a watch on this increasing flow of information, the other limitations to an information revolution are societal, namely low literacy; financial—limiting access to technology; and cultural—the overwhelmingly gendered nature of the virtual space, mirroring the public spaces. Women have lower rates of literacy, less ownership of mobile phones, and are less likely to use the internet. Naturally, this leads to fewer women being visible, let alone vocal. Women who do use the internet generally inhabit urban, elite or quasi-elite, upwardly mobile strata of society and their usage is often for a different purpose. Among Pakistani women, social networking becomes socializing and keeping in touch with friends and family; in comparison, more men seem to use social media to gather information and project influence. Across South Asia, this discrepancy represents the still gendered, indeed newly gendered norms of educational opportunities, material autonomy, digital training, and a discriminatory playing field.

Greater access and usage of smart phones has also resulted in greater online surveillance. Data protection laws were weak to begin with, but the 2016 Prevention of Electronic Crimes Act brought regulation of the internet. Its empowering of state authorities to gather and retain data has been seen as a weapon of mass surveillance, violating individual privacy, stifling civil liberties, and encouraging self-censorship. But these are existential matters for only a small top layer of society. Online trolling, the spread of misinformation, and propaganda wars waged by self-appointed or state-manufactured social media warriors are further concerns. These are global conversations and South Asia states are new players in the field.

At the same time, all of this is also part of a cultural reimagining that continues in the more widespread medium of the small screen. With the continued ban on films and television programmes from India (though those with access can watch these via online platforms), Pakistani audiences have been in thrall to Turkish productions. The popularity of programmes such as *Dirilis Ertugrul* ('Ertugrul's Resurrection'), a historical drama based on the life of a 13th-century Muslim whose son Osman Ghazi went on to establish the Ottoman Empire, is in turn utilized by Imran Khan's government for encouraging Islamic culture in contrast to what is perceived as morally questionable and Islamophobic entertainment from Hollywood and Bollywood. Such endorsements have reignited the old debate on what can be considered 'Pakistani' history and culture. Equally, there is accompanying anxiety as to how these global or pan-Islamic projects envelop and dilute local cultures. The programme has been accused of promoting violence, distorting history, and promoting a Turkish vision of pan-Islam, all of which ensured that it was banned in Saudi Arabia and the UAE. In Pakistan, such examples reinforce the shift to generally looking west, whether towards Turkey or the Gulf, for remaking Pakistani cultural identity, as opposed to the east, towards India, from which it has worked hard to divorce, distinguish, and distance itself. The pull towards India is diminishing rapidly with reduced interpersonal contact, especially since the two successive electoral victories of the fiercely Hindu nationalist Bharatiya Janata Party in India, the passing away of a generation with shared histories and memories, and the loosening of the threads of Hindustani language and pan-north Indian culture.

The links with Turkey, in any case, extend beyond cultural and religious kinship. Turkey was one of the first countries to recognize Pakistan in 1947 and, ironical in light of current goings-on, Jinnah looked to Mustafa Kemal Ataturk's secular Turkey as a model to emulate—a design that was also briefly revived by General Musharraf. More recently, the first Metrobus to be built in Pakistan, in Lahore, inaugurated in 2013, was a collaborative project between the Punjab and Turkish governments. While both Pakistan and Turkey have turned away from those mid-20th-century ideals of a modernizing and secularizing Islamic republic, this has opened up other possibilities for pan-religious and populist-nationalist inspirations.

Meanwhile, in a bid to make Pakistan attractive to the outside (western) world, the government has taken to promoting tourism, with the aim of changing the country's international image from 'terrorism to tourism' and making it an attractive tourist destination (Figure 17). The security situation today is comparatively more stable than the period 2009–14, one of intense activity by the Pakistan Taliban. Under successive army chiefs since Musharraf—Ashfaq Parvez Kayani and Raheel Sharif—the military, and the ISI (Inter-Services Intelligence), launched operations like Rah-e-Rast (in Swat) and Zarb-e-Azb (in Waziristan). From Karachi to Khyber, and from Wheeler to Wahhab, Pakistan remains a country of many difficulties and conflicts, but its hard image is being softened. Behind the motivation to change Pakistan's image lies the dire economic situation, the declining value of the Pakistani rupee and the billions of dollars owed to the

17. Truck Art, street in Lahore.

International Monetary Fund. Lifting visa restrictions and enabling electronic visas, along with a few well-placed 'foreign tourists' to publicize Brand Pakistan, are the latest government initiatives in this direction. The slow growth between 2014 and 2020 has been pegged back by the impact of the Covid-19 pandemic, but there is no denying the appeal and potential benefits of this attempt.

First, it seeks to capitalize on Pakistan's still unspoilt beauty in its northern areas (Khyber Pakhtunkhwa and Gilgit-Baltistan), by trying to re-establish some of the old (1960s) hippie trails, encouraging mountaineering and trekking in the Hindu Kush range, and expanding on establishments like the Malam Jabba ski resort dating from the 1980s in Swat Valley, much of which had been destroyed in 2008 by the Pakistan Taliban, after being declared 'un-Islamic'. Geologically, northern Pakistan is located on an active fault line, where the Indian and Eurasian tectonic plates meet, making it highly prone to earthquakes. In October 2005, an earthquake of 7.6 magnitude with its epicentre at Balakot devastated Azad Jammu and Kashmir and surrounding areas. It was one of the deadliest earthquakes in recent times, with an estimated death toll of 75,000–85,000 people. Relatedly, in July 2010, the Indus river valley saw flash floods, following a record-breaking monsoon, which brought untold misery to over a million people across all the major provinces who were displaced. These environmental challenges remain, especially given climate change, but equally important is the need to create an eco-friendly and sustainable infrastructure.

The second strand of tourism is multi-dimensional, people oriented, and has a diplomatic value. Three kilometres away from the India–Pakistan border, in Pakistani Punjab, is the gurdwara in Kartarpur, the final resting place of Guru Nanak, founder of the Sikh faith. On the other side, in Indian Punjab, is the bustling holy town of Dera Baba Nanak, again associated with the life and times of the guru. In November 2018, the governments of India and Pakistan took the momentous step of opening a corridor between these two gurdwaras, to enable visa-free travel for pilgrims—a long-standing desire of the Sikh communities of both countries. The development of this corridor was completed in time to mark the 550th birth anniversary of Guru Nanak in 2019. The Sikh community is concentrated in the Indian Punjab, but some of the most significant shrines associated with the faith are located in Pakistani Punjab, another sad outcome of India's Partition.

In recent times, these have been renovated to attract Sikh pilgrims from the diaspora and also from India too, but with the latter being at the mercy of the fluctuating relationship between the two governments. The Kartarpur corridor is therefore the kind of 'spiritual tourism' that the Pakistan government is keen to promote because it also shows the state in a positive light vis-à-vis its minorities, in addition to generating capital. However, by recreating these links with the Sikhs, the Pakistani state also runs the risk of reopening old accusations of propping up the Sikh separatist Khalistan Movement in India and abroad. On the other hand, in 2019, a statue of Maharaja Ranjit Singh (1780–1839) was installed near Lahore fort, as a tribute to that *Sher-e-Punjab* as a 'son of the soil'. Soon, perhaps not entirely unsurprisingly, it was subjected to vandalism, revealing the difficulty of untying the threads of religion, nation, and region. But, the issue of minorities, their political representation, inclusion in the national narrative, and place in the history of Pakistan continues to be central to the question: who is a Pakistani? This is especially important because the pool of people to choose from continues to shrink.

Overall, across the post-colonial world, a relative lack of political stability (due to both external and internal factors and historic and new) has hampered economic growth and social development in Pakistan. The country has weathered many storms and remains resilient, if slightly worn and fraying at the edges. Pakistan today may not be the 'promised land' to which many fled in August 1947, but after more than seventy years, it is certainly not 'a people without history' as the historian Faisal Devji suggests. That history, though, continues to be reworked and reimagined for a younger audience. The older, and some would argue more inclusive, memories have given way to newer, and more exclusionary, ambitions.

Timeline and key moments

1875	Muhammadan Anglo-Oriental College established in Aligarh.
1906	All-India Muslim League established in Dhaka.
1920	MAO College, Aligarh upgraded to Aligarh University.
1930	Muhammad Allama Iqbal gives his Allahabad Speech suggesting the creation of a separate Muslim state.
1933	Choudhry Rahmat Ali's pamphlet outlining a state of 'Pakistan'.
1940	AIML passes the Lahore Resolution—dubbed the Pakistan Resolution and two-nation theory.
1947	14 August—Partition of British India and creation of East and West Pakistan.
1948	September—the founding father Quaid-i-Azam dies.
1948	First war with India over disputed territory of Kashmir.
1949	Objectives Resolution by PM Liaquat Ali Khan is passed.
1951	October—PM Liaqat Ali Khan assassinated.
1956	Pakistan becomes an Islamic republic.
1958	October—martial law declared by General Ayub Khan.
1965	Fatima Jinnah loses the presidential elections, Ayub completes the second term. Second war with India over disputed territory of Kashmir.
1967	Pakistan People's Party founded by Zulfikar Ali Bhutto.
1969	Ayub Khan resigns and General Yahya Khan becomes president.

1970	November—devastating Bhola cyclone in East Pakistan, estimated 500,000 deaths.
1970	First democratic elections held in December (delayed due to Bhola). East Pakistan's Awami League wins.
1971	Yahya Khan resigns. Civil war in East Pakistan which turns into an Indo-Pakistan War. Secession of Bangladesh.
1972	Simla Agreement with India sets new Line of Control in Kashmir.
1973	Zulfikar Ali Bhutto becomes PM.
1974	Ban on Ahmadiyya calling themselves Muslims.
1977	General Zia ul-Haq declares martial law.
1979	April—Zulfikar Ali Bhutto hanged. Zia enacts the Hudood Ordinances. Abdus Salam becomes the first Pakistani to be awarded the Nobel Prize, for Physics.
1985	Martial law and ban on political parties lifted.
1986	Benazir Bhutto returns to Pakistan from exile to lead the PPP.
1988	August—General Zia dies in a plane crash. November—Benazir Bhutto's PPP wins general election.
1990	Bhutto dismissed on charges of corruption and incompetence. Nawaz Sharif becomes PM.
1992	Pakistan win Cricket World Cup under Imran Khan's captaincy.
1993	Sharif forced to resign; fresh elections bring Bhutto back to power.
1996	Bhutto government dismissed by President Leghari amid corruption charges.
1997	February—Sharif returns to power after PML wins elections.
1998	Chagai-I—first nuclear tests by Pakistan performed in Chagai District, Balochistan.
1999	May—Kargil war in Indian-held Kashmir. October—General Pervez Musharraf seizes power in a military coup.
2000	Nawaz Sharif sentenced to life imprisonment on hijacking and terrorism charges over his actions in the 1999 coup.

2001	July—Agra Summit starts. Musharraf and Indian PM Vajpayee hold talks.
2001	September—Musharraf backs the USA in its fight against terrorism. USA lifts some sanctions imposed after Pakistan's nuclear tests in 1998.
2002	First general elections since the 1999 military coup.
2003	Pakistan and India agree to resume direct air links, after a two-year ban.
2005	First bus service in sixty years operates between Muzaffarabad in Pakistani-administered Kashmir and Srinagar in Indian-controlled Kashmir. October—earthquake in Balakot and Azad Jammu and Kashmir with an estimated death toll of 75,000 people.
2007	March—Musharraf suspends Chief Justice Chaudhry, sparking a wave of protests.
2007	Benazir Bhutto returns to Pakistan after eight years' exile and Sharif returns after seven years' exile. Emergency lifted, banned civil rights and suspended constitution restored. Bhutto assassinated in December in Rawalpindi at a political rally.
2008	Yusuf Raza Gilani (PPP) becomes PM at head of coalition with Nawaz Sharif's PML (N) following parliamentary elections in February. August—Musharraf resigns after the two main governing parties agree to launch impeachment proceedings against him.
2008	Mumbai attacks in November; India hold Pakistan-based Lashkar-e-Taiba, an extremist terror organization, responsible.
2009	Sri Lankan cricket team attacked by militants in Lahore. All international cricket matches in Pakistan are suspended. Pakistan loses its status as hosts for the cricket World Cup 2011.
2010	Parliament approves constitutional reforms; Eighteenth Amendment transfers key powers from the president to the prime minister.

2011	Campaign to reform Pakistan's blasphemy law leads to the killing of Punjab Governor Salman Taseer in January and minorities minister Shahbaz Bhatti in March.
2011	May—Osama bin Laden is killed by American special forces in Abbottabad.
2012	Taliban gunmen attack a group of girls including Malala Yousafzai.
2012	Sharmeen Obaid-Chinoy becomes the Pakistani Academy Award winner for Best Documentary Short Subject for *Saving Face*.
2013	PML (N) wins parliamentary elections in May. Nawaz Sharif returns as PM.
2013	Suicide bombing at All Saints' Church, Walled City of Peshawar; 127 killed.
2014	Malala Yousafzai becomes the youngest person ever to win the Nobel Peace Prize.
2014	Taliban gunmen attack Army Public School in Peshawar killing 148 people—mostly children.
2015	China and Pakistan sign CPEC agreements worth billions of dollars.
2017	Suicide bombing inside the Shrine of Lal Shahbaz Qalandar in Sehwan, Sindh, a major Sufi shrine. The Islamic State claimes responsibility for the death of ninety people.
2017	March—Parliament passes a law allowing the country's Hindu minority to register their marriages for the first time since Partition from India in 1947. PM Sharif is forced to resign after being disqualified by the Supreme Court over corruption charges. He is convicted and given a jail sentence.
2018	General Elections in July. Imran Khan (PTI) becomes prime minister on a pledge to end corruption and dynastic politics.
2018	Asia Bibi, a Christian woman acquitted of blasphemy after eight years on death row, is freed from prison, prompting violent protests by Islamists.

Glossary

Ahmadiyya a movement whose followers believe that its founder Mirza Gulam Ahmad (*c.*1839–1908) was the Mahdi or promised messiah.

Aryans people who were speakers of the Proto Indo-European languages and thought to have settled in ancient Iran and the northern subcontinent.

Hindustani a group of mutually intelligible languages (Hind-Urdu) spoken in north-western India.

Muhajir migrant, especially used for those who migrated from UP in India in 1947.

Musalman a Muslim. Term used in colonial India and in vernaculars.

Naya Pakistan 'Naya' is 'New'. A conservative political slogan, denoting change, used by Imran Khan's PTI.

Sharia Islamic law; jurisprudence.

Shi'a followers of Caliph Ali, doctrinal sect in Islam.

Sufi Islamic mystic.

Sufism from the Arabic *tasawwuf*. Islamic mysticism but not a separate sect, rather a different interpretation. The belief that Islamic knowledge should be learned from the teacher.

Sunni literally a follower of the Prophetic tradition, a majority doctrinal sect.

Taliban plural of Talib/student.

References and further reading

Chapter 1: Progress of a dream

Ali, Tariq. *Can Pakistan Survive? The Death of a State*. Penguin Books, 1983.

Ali, Tariq. *The Duel: Pakistan on the Flight Path of American Power*. Simon and Schuster, 2009.

Baxter, Craig, ed. *Pakistan on the Brink: Politics, Economics, and Society*. Lexington Books, 2004.

Devji, Faisal. *Muslim Zion: Pakistan as a Political Idea*. Hurst Publishers, 2013.

Dhulipala, Venkat. *Creating a New Medina*. Cambridge University Press, 2015.

Fair, C. Christine. *Fighting to the End: The Pakistan Army's Way of War*. Oxford University Press, 2014.

Faiz, Faiz Ahmed, and Sheema Majeed. *Coming Back Home: Selected Articles, Editorials, and Interviews of Faiz Ahmed Faiz*. Oxford University Press, 2008.

Haqqani, Husain. *Pakistan: Between Mosque and Military*. Carnegie endowment, 2010.

Iqbal, Muhammad. 'Presidential Address to the Annual Session of the All-India Muslim League', Allahabad, 29 December 1930.

Jaffrelot, Christophe. *The Pakistan Paradox: Instability and Resilience*. Oxford University Press, 2015.

Jalal, Ayesha. *The State of Martial Rule*. University of Cambridge, 1990.

Jinnah, Muhammad Ali. 'Mr. Jinnah's Presidential Address to the Constituent Assembly of Pakistan'. 11 August 1947.

Jinnah, Muhammad Ali. 'Presidential Address by Muhammad Ali Jinnah to the Muslim League Lahore'. March 1940.

Jones, Owen Bennett. *Pakistan: Eye of the Storm*. Yale University Press, 2003.

Lieven, Anatol. *Pakistan: A Hard Country*. Public Affairs, 2012.

Rushdie, Salman. *Shame*. Vintage, 1995 (original 1983).

Shaikh, Farzana. *Making Sense of Pakistan*. Oxford University Press, 2018.

Siddiqa, Ayesha. *Military Inc.: Inside Pakistan's Military Economy*. Penguin Random House India, 2017.

Ziring, Lawrence. *Pakistan in the Twentieth Century: A Political History*. Oxford University Press, 1997.

Chapter 2: The ancient in the modern

Ahsan, Aitzaz. *The Indus Saga*. Roli Books Private Limited, 2005.

Albinia, Alice. *Empires of the Indus: The Story of a River*. John Murray, 2009.

Ali, Choudhry Rahmat. 'Now or Never: Are we to Live or Perish Forever?' Cambridge, 1933.

Chaffee, John W. *The Muslim Merchants of Premodern China: The History of a Maritime Asian Trade Diaspora, 750–1400*. Cambridge University Press, 2018.

Cunningham, Alexander. *The Ancient Geography of India*. Trübner and Co, 1871.

Hawkes, Jacquetta. *Mortimer Wheeler: Adventurer in Archaeology*. Weidenfeld and Nicolson, 1982.

Kenoyer, Jonathan Mark. *Ancient Cities of the Indus Valley Civilization*. Oxford University Press and American Institute of Pakistan Studies, 1998.

Lahiri, Nayanjot, ed. *The Decline and Fall of the Indus Civilization*. Permanent Black, 2000.

Lahiri, Nayanjot. *Finding Forgotten Cities: How the Indus Civilization was Discovered*. Hachette UK, 2012.

Malik, Iftikhar Haider. *The History of Pakistan*. Greenwood Publishing Group, 2008.

Marshall, John. *A Guide to Taxila*. Delhi, 1936; reprint Cambridge University Press, 2013.

Mill, James. *The History of British India*. Baldwin, Cradock and Joy, 1817.

Singh, Upinder. *A History of Ancient and Early Medieval India: From the Stone Age to the 12th Century (PB)*. Pearson Education India, 2009.

Thapar, Romila. *A History of India*, Volume One. Penguin UK, 1990-reprint.

Trautmann, Thomas R. *Kautilya and the Arthasastra: A Statistical Investigation of the Authorship and Evolution of the Text*. EJ Brill, 1971.

Wheeler, R. E. M. *My Archaeological Mission to India and Pakistan*. Thames and Hudson, 1976.

Wheeler, R. E. M. *The Indus Civilization: Supplementary Volume of the Cambridge History of India*. Cambridge University Press, 1953.

Chapter 3: Towards the idea of Pakistan

Ahmad, Sir Sayyid. *The Present State of Indian Politics, Consisting of Speeches and Letters Reprinted from the 'Pioneer'*. Indian Patriotic Assn., 1888. <http://www.columbia.edu/itc/mealac/pritchett/00islamlinks/txt_sir_sayyid_meerut_1888.html>

Ali, M. Mohar. 'Hunter's Indian Musalmans: A Re-examination of its Background'. *Journal of the Royal Asiatic Society* 112, no. 1 (1980): 30–51.

Ali, Syed Ameer. *The Spirit of Islam: A History of the Evolution and Ideals of Islam*. Cosmo, Inc., 2010 (originally published 1891).

Ansari, Sarah. *Life after Partition: Migration, Community and Strife in Sindh, 1947–1962*. Oxford University Press, 2005.

Bangash, Yaqoob Khan. *A Princely Affair: The Accession and Integration of the Princely States of Pakistan, 1947–1955*. Oxford University Press, 2015.

Basu, Shrabani. *For King and Another Country: Indian Soldiers on the Western Front, 1914–18*. Bloomsbury, 2015.

Chatterji, Bankim Chandra. *Anandamath*. Orient paperbacks, 2019.

Cohen, Stephen P. *The Idea of Pakistan*. Brookings Institution Press, 2004.

Copland, Ian. 'The Integration of the Princely States: A "bloodless revolution"?' *South Asia: Journal of South Asian Studies* 18, no. s1 (1995): 131–51.

Eaton, Richard M. *India in the Persianate Age: 1000–1765*. Penguin, 2019.

Hali, Altaf Hussain. A translation and critical introduction by
    Christopher Shackle and Javed Majeed (Oxford University Press,
    1997). <http://www.columbia.edu/itc/mealac/pritchett/00urdu/
    hali/musaddas/index.html>.

Iqbal, Muhammad. Full transcript of Iqbal's speech: Sir Muhammad
    Iqbal's 1930 Presidential Address to the 25th Session of the
    All-India Muslim League Allahabad, 29 December 1930.
    <http://www.columbia.edu/itc/mealac/pritchett/00islamlinks/
    txt_iqbal_1930.html>.

Jalal, Ayesha. *The Sole Spokesman: Jinnah, the Muslim League and
    the Demand for Pakistan*. Cambridge University Press, 1994.

Qasmi, Ali Usman, and Megan Eaton Robb, eds. *Muslims against the
    Muslim League*. Cambridge University Press, 2017.

Robinson, Francis. *Separatism Among Indian Muslims: The Politics of
    the United Provinces' Muslims, 1860–1923*. Cambridge University
    Press, 2007.

Shackle, Christopher. 'Making Punjabi Literary History'. *Sikh
    Religion, Culture and Ethnicity*. Routledge, 2013: 107–27.

Shackle, Christopher. 'Urdu Poetry as a Vehicle for Islamic
    Re-Expression'. *Religious Perspectives in Modern Muslim and
    Jewish Literatures* (2004): 13.

Stephens, Ian. *Pakistan: Old Country New Nation*. Penguin
    Books, 1964.

Wilson Hunter, William. *The Indian Musalmans: Are They Bound in
    Conscience to Rebel Against the Queen?* Trübner and
    Company, 1871.

Chapter 4: Consolidation and fragmentation

Ansari, Sarah. *Life after Partition: Migration, Community and Strife
    in Sindh, 1947–1962*. Oxford University Press, 2005.

Jalal, Ayesha. *The State of Martial Rule: The Origins of Pakistan's
    Economy of Defence*. Cambridge University Press, 1990.

Jinnah, Muhammad Ali. 'Address by Muhammad Ali Jinnah, Governor
    General of Pakistan, in Dacca, East Pakistan'. 21 March 1948.

Khan, Nichola, ed. *Cityscapes of Violence in Karachi: Publics and
    Counter Publics*. Oxford University Press, 2017.

Khan, Nichola. *Mohajir Militancy in Pakistan: Violence and
    Transformation in the Karachi Conflict*. Routledge, 2010.

Kudaisya, Gyanesh, and Tan Tai Yong. *The Aftermath of Partition in
    South Asia*. Routledge, 2004.

Siddiqa, Ayesha. *Military Inc.: Inside Pakistan's Military Economy*. Penguin Random House India, 2017.

Singh, Khushwant, 'Pakistan, India and the Bomb'. *The New York Times*, 1 July 1979.

Spate, Oskar Hermann Khristian, et al. *India and Pakistan*. Methuen, 1967.

Talbot, Ian. *Pakistan: A Modern History*. Hurst, 2009.

Weinraub, Bernard. 'Pakistan Admits that Bangladesh Exists as Nation'. *The New York Times*, 23 February 1974.

Zamindar, Vazira Fazila-Yacoobali. *The Long Partition and the Making of Modern South Asia: Refugees, Boundaries, Histories*. Columbia University Press, 2007.

Chapter 5: Building the land of the pure

Ali, Tariq. *Can Pakistan Survive? The Death of a State*. Penguin Books, 1983.

Haq, Khadija, ed. *Economic Growth with Social Justice: Collected Writings of Mahbub ul Haq*. Oxford University Press, 2018.

Ispahani, Farahnaz. *Purifying the Land of the Pure: Pakistan's Religious Minorities*. Harper Collins, 2015.

Khan, Ayesha. *The Women's Movement in Pakistan: Activism, Islam and Democracy*. Bloomsbury Publishing, 2018.

Long, Roger D., Gurharpal Singh, Yunas Samad, and Ian Talbot, eds. *State and Nation-Building in Pakistan: Beyond Islam and Security*. Routledge, 2015.

Qasmi, Ali Usman. *The Ahmadis and the Politics of Religious Exclusion in Pakistan*. Anthem Press, 2014.

Shaheed, Farida, and Khawar Mumtaz, eds. *Women of Pakistan: Two Steps Forward, One Step Back?* Zed Book, 1987.

Chapter 6: Visualizing the land of the pure

Ali, Khan, and Ali Nobil Ahmad. *Cinema and Society: Film and Social Change in Pakistan*. Oxford University Press, 2016.

Ayres, Alyssa. *Speaking like a State: Language and Nationalism in Pakistan*. Cambridge University Press, 2009.

Bhutto, Fatima, 'How Pakistan Banned a New Drama—and Put it up for an Oscar'. *The Guardian*, 22 January 2021. <https://www.theguardian.com/film/2021/jan/22/how-pakistan-banned-a-new-drama-then-put-it-up-for-an-oscar>.

Brown, Louise. *The Dancing Girls of Lahore: Selling Love and Saving Dreams in Pakistan's Pleasure District*. Harper Perennial, 2006.

Gandhi, Mahatma, Mahomed Ali Jinnah, and Chakravarti Rajagopalachari. *Gandhi–Jinnah Talks: Text of Correspondence and Other Relevant Matter, July–October, 1944*. Hindustan Times, 1944.

Gazdar, Mushtaq. *Pakistan Cinema, 1947–1997*. Oxford University Press, 1997.

Jalal, Ayesha. *The Struggle for Pakistan*. Harvard University Press, 2014.

Maher, Sanam. *A Woman Like Her: The Sensational Life and Death of Qandeel Baloch*. Bloomsbury, 2019.

Malik, Iftikhar Haider. *Culture and Customs of Pakistan*. Greenwood Publishing Group, 2006.

Rumi, Raza. *Being Pakistani: Society, Culture and the Arts*. Harper Collins, 2018.

Shahid, Khaldun. 'Bulldozing History'. *The Friday Times*, 20 November 2015 (last accessed 10 March 2020, <https://www. thefridaytimes.com/bulldozing-history/>).

Toor, Saadia. 'A National Culture for Pakistan: The Political Economy of a Debate'. *Inter-Asia Cultural Studies* 6, no. 3 (2005): 318–40.

Toor, Sadia. *The State of Islam*. Pluto, 2011.

Yaqin, Amina. 'Variants of Cultural Nationalism in Pakistan: A Reading of Faiz Ahmad Faiz, Jamil Jalibi, and Fahmida Riaz'. In Kelly Pemberton and Michael Nijhawan, eds, *Shared Idioms, Sacred Symbols, and the Articulation of Identities in South Asia*. Routledge, 2009.

Chapter 7: The world outside

Ahmed, Zahid Shahab. 'Impact of the China–Pakistan Economic Corridor on Nation-Building in Pakistan'. *Journal of Contemporary China* 28, no. 117 (2019): 400–14.

Ali, Nasreen, Virinder S. Kalra, and Salman Sayyid. *A Postcolonial People: South Asians in Britain*. Hurst & Company, 2006.

Ansari, Humayun. *The Infidel Within: Muslims in Britain since 1800*. Oxford University Press, 2018.

Anwar, Muhammad. *The Myth of Return: Pakistanis in Britain*. Heinemann Educational Books, 1979.

Ballard, Roger. 'The Political Economy of Migration: Pakistan, Britain, and the Middle East'. In John Eades, ed., *Migrants, Workers and the Social Order*, Tavistock, 1987.

Chopra, Surendra. 'Afghan Pakistan Relations: The Pakhtoonistan Issue'. *The Indian Journal of Political Science* 35, no. 4 (1974): 310–31.

Kalra, Virinder S. *From Textile Mills to Taxi Ranks: Experiences of Migration, Labour and Social Change*. Routledge, 2000, reissued 2019.

Khan, Shaharyar M., and Ali Khan. *Cricket Cauldron: The Turbulent Politics of Sport in Pakistan*. Bloomsbury Publishing, 2013.

Nasr, Sayed Vali Reza. 'The Rise of Sunni Militancy in Pakistan: The Changing Role of Islamism and the Ulama in Society and Politics'. *Modern Asian Studies* 34, no. 1 (2000): 139–80.

Osborne, Peter. *Wounded Tiger: A History of Cricket in Pakistan*. Simon and Schuster, 2015.

Rushdie, Salman. *Shalimar: The Clown*. Vintage Books, 2005.

Sardar, Ziauddin. *A Person of Pakistani Origins*. Oxford University Press, 2018.

Sardar, Ziauddin. Interview with Mustafa Nazir Ahmad in The News on Sunday, 23 November 2008, <https://ziauddinsardar.com/interviews/reformist>.

Shamsie, Kamila. 'Strong Arms: The Story of Pakistan Women's Cricket'. *The Cricket Monthly*, 16 October 2019.

Chapter 8: Looking backwards, going forward?

Adeney, Katharine. 'How to Understand Pakistan's Hybrid Regime: The Importance of a Multidimensional Continuum'. *Democratization*, 24 no. 1 (2017): 119–37.

Devji, Faisal. *The Muslim Zion*. Hurst, 2013.

Human Development Reports, UN, <http://hdr.undp.org/en/countries/profiles/PAK>.

Khan, Imran. Prime Minister's Address to the Nations. Prime Minister's Office, 19 August 2018, <https://pmo.gov.pk/press_release_detailes.php?pr_id=2395>.

Maqsood, Ammara. *The New Pakistani Middle Class*. Harvard University Press, 2017.

Multidimensional Poverty in Pakistan. UNDP, Pakistan 20 June 2016. <https://www.pk.undp.org/content/pakistan/en/home/library/development_policy/Multidimensional-Poverty-in-Pakistan.html>.

Qasmi, Ali Usman. 'Making Sense of Naya Pakistan—I.' *The Friday Times*, 7 September 2018, <https://www.thefridaytimes.com/making-sense-of-naya-pakistan-i/>.

Index

For the benefit of digital users, indexed terms that span two pages (e.g., 52–53) may, on occasion, appear on only one of those pages.

ISLAMIC HISTORY
A Very Short Introduction
Adam J. Silverstein

Does history matter? This book argues not that history matters, but that Islamic history does. This *Very Short Introduction* introduces the story of Islamic history; the controversies surrounding its study; and the significance that it holds - for Muslims and for non-Muslims alike. Opening with a lucid overview of the rise and spread of Islam, from the seventh to twenty first century, the book charts the evolution of what was originally a small, localised community of believers into an international religion with over a billion adherents. Chapters are also dedicated to the peoples - Arabs, Persians, and Turks - who shaped Islamic history, and to three representative institutions - the mosque, jihad, and the caliphate - that highlight Islam's diversity over time.

'The book is extremely lucid, readable, sensibly organised, and wears its considerable learning, as they say, 'lightly'.'

BBC History Magazine